THE FIRST TEN YEARS

Also by Joseph Fink

The Faceless Old Woman Who Secretly Lives in Your Home
Alice Isn't Dead
It Devours!
The Buying of Lot 37
Who's a Good Boy?
Mostly Void, Partially Stars
Great Glowing Coils of the Universe
Welcome to Night Vale
The Halloween Moon

THE FIRST TEN YEARS

Two Sides of the Same Love Story

Joseph Fink
and
Meg Bashwiner

HARPER ● PERENNIAL

NEW YORK ● LONDON ● TORONTO ● SYDNEY ● NEW DELHI ● AUCKLAND

HARPER ● PERENNIAL

HarperCollins books may be purchased for educational, business, or sales promotional use. For information, please email the Special Markets Department at SPsales@harpercollins.com.

FIRST EDITION

Designed by Jen Overstreet

Library of Congress Cataloging-in-Publication Data has been applied for.

ISBN 978-0-06-302725-1

21 22 23 24 25   LSC   10 9 8 7 6 5 4 3 2 1

For our daughter,
who spoils the ending of this book on page one

THIS BOOK CHRONICLES THE first ten years of our relationship, from each of our points of view.

We wrote these chapters in 2019 without consulting one another beforehand.

Any discrepancies in fact or memory are accidental and fiercely disagreed upon.

THE FIRST TEN YEARS

2009

Joseph

2009 STILL FEELS LIKE present tense. A decade passes so quickly.

We met in the East Village, selling tickets for a downtown per-formance art collective called the New York Neo-Futurists, working in a tiny cubicle of a box office where the inner wall was a corkboard littered with programs for shows that had closed years before. Meg was interning with the Neo-Futurists, and I had recently auditioned for them and not been cast. Having nowhere else to go in New York, I subsequently showed up every weekend to their show, volunteering at their box office so that I wouldn't have to pay for tickets. The crash of 2008 had left me with few savings and no job.

We were twenty-two and full of the posturing performance that substitutes for personality at that age. In a person's early twenties, the human being who eventually will form naturally with time has to be hastily scraped together from the shaky models of movies and social media. Meg was a constant smoker then, and so my first impression of her was a rolling wave of cigarette smell. My sense of smell is sensitive, and neither I nor anyone in my family ever smoked, so it set that first meeting on edge. But she also was clearly smart and determined and so entirely different from most people I had ever known, a slice of Jersey in my—until then—entirely Californian life. I didn't quite know what to make of her. But then I was such an uncertain mess at that age that I didn't know what to make of myself, either. I don't remember us getting along well the first night we met, but I think we both knew that the conflict was as fake as the version of ourselves we were performing. There were deeper, quieter versions of us waiting to unfurl, and it was in those silent places that the heat between us lingered.

The night we met, we went with the cast of the performance we had been selling tickets for to a restaurant in the East Village that doesn't exist anymore. Most restaurants in the East Village don't exist anymore. During the evening, it somehow came up that Meg loved seafood and I hate even the smell of seafood. Kevin R. Free, a member of the Neo-Futurists and a future member of the *Welcome to Night Vale* cast, laughed and said, "Well, you two will never have sex."

We would tell that story many times in the future, and Meg would always end it the same way.

"And he was right."

New York in 2009 was teetering over the gap between the mythology of a thriving city for dreamers and the reality of the worst economic collapse in eighty years. I had no job and no prospect of one for six months after moving to the city. There were job fairs in Herald Square where the line to even get into the building was an hour or two long, all for the privilege of being the one thousandth resume deposited on one of the eight tables inside. It was clear to all of us that the future of our generation had been gambled away by the previous genera-tions, and now there was nothing left for us. After several months, I found a minimum-wage temp job at a refrigeration chemical company a ninety-minute subway commute from Windsor Terrace, the quiet, quasi-suburban neighborhood in Brooklyn that was the most central area I could afford. I remember being ecstatic that I found that job. I was let go after two weeks. There were few companies hiring, not when they could grab temps, throw a few tasks at them, and discard them as easily as the trash bags full of resumes going out to the curb every day. It was in the wake of this disaster that Meg and I met. It didn't feel like an unhappy time, exactly. I remember it fondly. But we were survivors of a shipwreck floating on adjacent debris, and that must have defined how we related to each other.

Meg and I were only friends. I was in the messy process of ending the relationship I had been in since I was fourteen. I had never been an adult outside of that relationship and didn't know what that even looked like, but I knew that I definitely needed to be single for a while. So, I resisted any feeling that might have been there with Meg. But that feeling in retrospect was undeniable.

Looking back at Facebook posts, at a time when people our age used Facebook, before it became primarily a place to radicalize boomers, there is an almost aggressive internet flirtation between the two of us. Like many people, we were doing online what we hadn't found a way to do in real life. Meg went through and liked every Facebook status I had ever posted, which is a form of flirtation that would be difficult to explain to previous generations. What new forms of flirtation will young people invent in the future? Truly bold frontiers of science await.

I would regularly publicly proclaim my interest in being single, as a defense mechanism for how badly that was going for me. The truth was I had no understanding of how to be single, and no model in my life for how that worked. My parents met on the first day of their freshman year of college, sitting at the same table in the dining hall. My aunt and uncle had been together since they were thirteen years old. There was a reason I had been in the same relationship from fourteen years old until I attempted a clean break by moving across the country: my natural state was monogamy. Still is, I guess.

One night, in May of 2009, Meg and I ate at a fancy-ish Mexican restaurant off Houston Street that I think since closed and had its space filled by a Chipotle. I was eating a lot of Mexican food at the time because I missed the West Coast. And I was always disappointed because it is nearly impossible to get decent Mexican food in New

York City. (Longtime residents of New York will always insist that this isn't true, and to prove it they'll give you the name of their go-to place, and you'll go there and the food will be bad to mediocre. My theory is that New York has a reputation for great food not because its food is noticeably better, but because the people that live there have shrunk their expectations and don't eat outside the city much. But I get away from the romance.) Meg considered me from across the table, between us our little lava stone bowl of guacamole that is for some reason a mandatory element of every New York City Mexican meal. There was a fission there, but when you're twenty-two there is a fission everywhere. Your body has more energy than it will ever have from that point forward, and you project that energy out onto the world. That is why, in retrospect, the world feels brighter, more vivid, and more real when we are young. The world fades as we fade. So, my experience of the city that rainy spring was a crackling, humming one.

Meg eyed me from across the table. We were just friends, after all. Just friends who spent most of our time together and regularly ate meals together, but just friends. She was quiet for a moment, holding my gaze, and then she said, "I just realized something about you."

"What?"

"I can't tell you."

She had realized she liked me, of course. I knew that, of course. She knew I knew that. We both pretended we didn't know it. We finished our food. I went to my new apartment in Chelsea, the one I moved to because living in Windsor Terrace did not feel enough like the "city life." I slept in the only bedroom, and my roommate, an unemployed photographer a few decades my senior, slept in the living room. Meg and I were sliding down a slope toward an ending we both knew was coming, but both pretended we didn't. Or maybe at the time I truly didn't know. It is impossible to consider the past divorced from my knowledge of how it turned out.

April turned to May turned to June, and the air went sticky. It was my first summer in the city, where the garbage rots in double time but the parks become intoxicating in the evening, laughing gaggles of people hanging together on the grass and on the concrete. That first summer I remember it rained constantly. I had never seen storms like that. My native Southern California does occasionally get rain, despite our reputation. But New York storms kick down your door, hit you with a firehose, and then are gone in minutes. California rain nurtures, New York rain roughs up.

In early June, some high school friends of Meg's were playing at the Bitter End in the West Village, and she suggested we could go see the show together, and then she could stay the night so she wouldn't have to drive back to her parents' house in Jersey. She showed up at my door all elaborate makeup and straightened hair, completely beautiful and smelling of cigarettes and probably wearing her ex-boyfriend's fedora, which she wore constantly that spring. I looked at her and I knew. But I didn't know that I knew. There was a lot of knowing but not knowing I knew when I was younger, and probably now too. We ate dinner with my roommate, got uncomfortably high, and then went to the show. On top of our high, we got drunk. The world went jangly. I took a picture of the graffiti-filled bathroom of the Bitter End and it was only by later checking the date on that blurry photo in my silver flip phone that we would be able to confirm our anniversary. Yes, we count this as the start, and why not?

On the way home, Meg wanted to pet a police horse. I wanted to be nowhere near the police. The streets staggered and swayed, and then we were on Seventh Avenue, across the street from my apartment, and she stopped me.

"I like you," she said.

"I'm not a good person to like," I said, which came out of the script of some macho fantasy of being single in New York and was, it transpired, not remotely true. But the urge to kiss her was irresistible. So much about her was irresistible. The next morning, I gave her some money to help with the morning-after pill.

A day later I would write on Facebook, "36 hours and a long shower and I still have a play written on my arm." Ten years later we would read that and not remember what it was in reference to, but it sure sounds like us.

The summer of 2009 was the summer when my fragile ability to cope finally deserted me. I don't know what combination of factors sparked the change, but there are any number of possibilities. Six months earlier, I had moved away from my parents' house for the first time post college, when the move is no longer a temporary adventure but an understanding that in all likelihood you will never come back. I was living on the opposite coast from the one I knew, in a city I wasn't entirely sure I wanted to live in. I had my first full-time, non-temp post-college adult job, a low-level customer service position at a pre-paid debit card company that I absolutely hated. I was starting a new relationship. And my father was dying, without any clear indication of whether we had a year left or ten years or two days. (As it turns out, we had two years exactly from that summer.)

All these factors piled up, and I collapsed under them. That was the summer when air stopped working for me. I would gasp and gasp but my lungs would never fill. On a crowded street in Manhattan, I would drown. I saw a doctor once who gave me tranquilizers that only made me more anxious. I saw a therapist once who then spent the rest of the year hounding me about the amount I owed him, so that was overall a net negative. There was an ambulance ride and ER visit after I was convinced I was having a heart attack at work. Anxiety hasn't exactly gotten easier in the ten years I've lived with it since, but it was a stranger to me that summer, and a threatening stranger at that.

One night in July, a month after that first night, I called Meg mid–panic attack, and she drove in from New Jersey. She brought me the DVDs of the first two seasons of *Saturday Night Live*, and a box of chocolate-covered strawberries. I took the bakery string from that box, cut it in half, and we tied the pieces around each of our wrists, a semi-ironic friendship bracelet to remind me of when Meg was there for me exactly when and how I needed her to be. We've worn matching bakery string around our wrists ever since. The string is replaced occasionally as it wears out. Sometimes we remember to do that on our anniversary, but often we forget, and just do it whenever it is needed. Romantic gestures are great, but you don't need to build a life around them.

I'm very particular about what goes on my body. I hate wearing ties. I don't like the feeling of jewelry on me, so I don't wear my wedding ring. I'd probably be happiest in a nudist colony. But I do wear a bakery string around my wrist and always will. To me, that is the marker that means something. Unlike a wedding ring, it's something we made for ourselves.

Meg's family had a small house down on Long Beach Island off the coast of New Jersey. Growing up in Southern California, my images of East Coast beaches were based on, probably, images of New England. Rocks and lighthouses and cold waves breaking against snowy shores. It blew my mind to encounter fine sand and warm water. She took me there that first summer. It was just the two of us. We had piña coladas made from a packet mix bought at a liquor store off island, and in the morning she made us bagel sandwiches bulging with egg and cheese and Taylor Ham, a New Jersey specialty that is as good a testament to New Jersey as anything else: simple, delicious, and with absolutely no pretense. After going back to work at the prepaid debit card job in Manhattan, I would get egg-and-cheese bagel sandwiches in the mornings from the bodega by my work because they reminded me of her. As a result, I gained a good deal of weight, literally becoming fat on the memory of her.

Long Beach Island also became the only place that summer where

I wasn't a continual walking panic attack. My fear was of death, and for some reason it felt impossible that I would die in a place that beautiful, which is as rational a belief as any I had during that time. Looking back, it was likely that it wasn't the island but the woman attached to it that felt like the stability the rest of my life was missing. She and the sunshine and the outdoor shower with an open beer and the warm waves all became one unified thing, and that thing was the start of my life on the East Coast, and so the start of my adult life altogether.

In October, I decided to get my first tattoo to celebrate my first year in New York City. My plan was I'd get a tattoo for every major milestone in my life. That idea was pretty quickly scrapped, and my current plan is I get a tattoo every few years when I get the urge, which is much more doable. I spent days researching and found an artist in the East Village who had an impressive portfolio. Meg volunteered to go with me, and so the two of us wandered around the neighborhood waiting for my appointment time. I was all nerves, my baseline anxiety providing a foundation for the towering edifice of first-time tattoo jitters, and so Meg did her best to distract me. There was a wall on the street that said "Post No Bills," and we started thinking of all the Bills we could post on that wall. Bill Clinton. Bill Nye. Once we ran out of famous Bills we started improvising. Billiam Shakespeare. Billiam H. Macy. Bob the Bill-der. Meg bought a large bag of frosted animal crackers with the promise that I could eat the whole thing once the tattoo was done.

"So how long have you been together," asked the tattoo artist, a broad and bearded man named Chad who was busy stabbing the state flowers of California and New York (a poppy and a rose) into my forearm.

"Oh, we're not . . . it's not . . . we're just . . ." we mumbled, and Chad rolled his eyes.

"It's like that, huh?" he said.

Chad saw right through us, or, more specifically, he saw right through me. After the tattoo, I ate the entire bag of frosted animal crackers, and the next morning Meg helped me wash the tattoo for the first time.

That fall I finally gave up on my stupid idea of being single and made what was obvious official. Meg and I became an exclusive couple. My parents visited that December. I'm glad of so many things, but that Meg and my father got to know each other for a while before he died is one of them. She remembers him too, so she can understand my grief. But that was all before, back when he was only dying and not yet gone. We gave them tours of the East Village and of Chelsea. We went to markets and to our favorite Thai restaurant on Seventh Avenue and we saw *A Little Night Music* starring Angela Lansbury in her last Broadway role. On the High Line, an elevated train track turned public park on the West Side of Manhattan, Meg and I walked through the snow.

Behind us, my mom took a photo that still hangs in her hallway. In it, we wrap our arms around each other, bundled in thick winter coats. Our faces aren't visible, but our heads lean toward each other, talking quietly with the urgent conspiracy of early love. Hanging over us is a billboard, advertising a whiskey or else a car or else perfume. The text on the billboard says: "All I need is all I've got."

Meg

I DON'T REMEMBER THE exact specific details about waking up the morning of Joseph's and my first date. Probable stimuli were the four walls of my childhood bedroom, a floor covered in a mix of dirty and clean clothes, and a ceiling with a dusty swirling fan. I graduated college the summer before and promptly moved in with my parents in Jersey. I had majored in Make Pretend (read: Theater Arts), and the economy had just collapsed and they were generously willing to have me, so I boomeranged right back home.

Lots of people my age were in the same boat and completely miserable, but luckily for me, living with my parents was . . . all right. My parents were the "cool parents" who treated me and my friends like adults. We could be ourselves around them. They didn't give me shit about staying out late or smoking too much weed. It was the general annoyance of not having anything of my own and of being in a holding pattern that kept circling adulthood but was continually unable to land that frustrated me. Things were tough at the beginning before I had a job, and I was just sitting around every day making the house messy by depressively existing in it. Eventually, I settled into the millennial must-have lifestyle of two or more jobs cobbled together to still not make enough money to afford NYC rent. As a result, I was rarely home to piss my parents off by abandoning my shoes in a walkway or leaving the front porch ashtray overflowing.

I woke up the morning of our first date as me, a desperately lonely twenty-three-year-old with lots of feelings. I was sad a lot, depressed a lot. I was pining for the life I had left behind the year before, my senior year in college. It was a hard fall going from really thriving in an educational and social environment to being slammed into the reality of half a life back in the suburbs with an unclear path. I worked a day job in insurance claims and a night job interning with the New York Neo-Futurists, an experimental theater company in NYC, where I had met and befriended Joseph a few months prior to this day. He had been on vacation for the past two weeks. While he was away I missed him, and that missing him inspired me to decide that I liked him enough to risk our friendship and to make a play for him. I had a lot of friends and zero boyfriends. Today was going to be the day.

I texted with Joseph about our plans for the night as I drank iced coffee and smoked weed sitting on a beach chair in my parents' garage. We planned to see my friend from high school's band. Then after the show I would sleep over at Joseph's apartment, because I was bridge-and-tunnel trash and it would be too late for me to drive home. He didn't have a couch or an air mattress or anything, so the plan was for me to just sleep in his bed, like single adult people with a history of flirtation do.

I began my physical preparations for our date. My beauty regimen consisted of straightening the humidity waves out of my box-dyed red hair, putting on too much gold eye shadow, a ring of black eyeliner around my bloodshot eyes, and mismatched concealer on my adult acne.

I wore fake silver jewelry that I was low-key allergic to. Hives are beauty. Then on a slutty whim, I put in my tongue piercing, which I thought had closed up but actually, after the application of brute force, had not. I selected the ring with the image of the Virgin Mary on the stud, ordered from the internet for $24 while I was still in college and I had a total of $42 in my bank account. If you needed a precise example of who I was at this time in my life, let this detail be that example.

I dressed in some sort of late-aughts Jersey-party-girl-trying-to-catch-a-dick outfit, complete with black lace-bottom leggings and a miniskirt. I finished the ensemble with my black Steve Madden high-heeled cowboy boots, as they were my signature at the time. I thought I looked dope as hell. I had no idea I would think back upon these clothes as I put them in the giveaway pile and feel a sticky combination of deep shame and confident pride. Yes, I could have passed for a mildly goth roommate from the TV show *Jersey Shore*, whose wardrobe was a mishmash of sale items from the juniors section at Marshalls and a smattering of "sold as is" capsule pieces acquired from Hot Topic, but this was *my* look. I didn't have much agency over my sputtering-to-a-start adulthood, but I could wear cowboy boots anywhere that I wanted. They gave me the confidence to loudly stomp through this uncertain time in my life. No one fucks with a cowboy.

Now that I was coated in my Lycra, nickel-plated, and pleather suit of armor and feeling good, I drove my Volkswagen Golf into the city from Jersey. I sat in bumper-to-bumper traffic on the Lincoln Tunnel Helix while smoking Camel Light Wides and presumably listening and slurring along to John Mayer because of my oversize tongue ring. I vividly remember parking the next block over from Joseph's new apartment in a choice spot. I am a proud parallel parker and sleuth for free parking in New York City; this remains unchanged. This is also one of the few details about this date that I am not embarrassed to share.

I walked up to his apartment at the corner of Sixteenth Street and Seventh Avenue. I had been to his apartment several times before. I helped him move into it from his place in Brooklyn. Helping someone move is the ultimate early-twenties flirtation. His super-intense doorman grilled me about who I was and where I was going. This would continue every time I entered his apartment for the next year. He would yell the apartment number at me, "2E! 2E! 2E!" and I would reply, "Yes, 2E, thank you." The doorman was also named Joseph, which likely aided in the continued confusion. Joseph the doorman eventually let me upstairs to Joseph the object of my desire's apartment, my high-heeled boots clicking across the tiled hallway counting down the final moments of the time in my life that was firmly before our relationship.

Joseph opened the door and immediately said, "You straightened your hair." My spot was instantly blown up; he caught me making an effort to be desirable. I steered into it and responded by showing him my Virgin Mary tongue ring, to really double down. Because hey, if he can see your cards, why not throw them on the table and show off how good your hand is? This exchange occurred in the hallway. He eventually let me inside.

We caught up a bit. He was bronzed from his recent vacation to Hawaii. I had never been. It seemed like a magical place that I would never get to go to because it was outside of the Tri-State area. We drank whiskey and smoked some weed with his very strange, middle-aged, out-of-work-fashion-photographer roommate/landlord.

Joseph played the guitar for us. He didn't know any John Mayer or DMB—the only covers he knew were Leonard Cohen. I was experiencing a paradigm shift, this was not the status quo. Every boy-with-a-guitar crush I had ever had knew those sweet, sweet sing-along jams. "What do you mean you don't know 'Crash Into Me' or 'Your Body Is a Wonderland'?" I said out loud. *Do you play guitar just because you like music and not just to get laid? WEIRD!* I thought to myself.

At this point in my life, I was still fresh out of college. I could really drink. I also smoked weed every day at the time, so I was used to its effects. Joseph, on the other hand, was not a party-girl pothead and had a little trouble keeping up with me. I remember him repeating "I am very intoxicated" over and over again. I thought it best we get on with our night and get him some fresh air. So the three of us—Joseph, his aged sad roommate, and I—took a cab downtown to the Bitter End on Bleecker Street to see this band.

We were in one of those cinematic New York City moments as we rode down Seventh Avenue in a yellow taxi to the West Village.

The city was all lit up and filled with people who were making their way out of their winter hibernation and onto the warmed sidewalks to bathe in the gentle humidity and faint garbage smell of the late-spring weekend night.

When we pulled up to the Bitter End, his roommate stayed in the taxi, stating that he was too drunk and high to be around people. We hadn't realized this at the time, but his roommate only ever left the house once a day to go to the gym and the vitamin store. We were still pleasantly unaware that he was a shut-in who would grow to hate and resent our youth.

We rocked up to the bar and I ordered a drink, probably like a fucking Bacardi and Diet Coke, as that was the unofficial drink of the times for North Jersey party girls, the close second place being Red Bull and Vodka (it is a miracle I survived). I ordered water for Joseph because I wanted him to not throw up and ruin my plans to pounce on him later like a jungle cat.

I saw my friend from high school, and he was surprised and touched that I came to his show. I was mostly using the show as a badge to show off to Joseph that I was cool, that I knew people who did things, I knew people who knew John Mayer covers on guitar. I think we stayed for his set? It was unmemorable, which could have been due to the content, my nervousness about making a move on Joseph, or the Bacardi and Diets. Likely the combo.

We decided to walk back to Joseph's apartment to enjoy the finally comfortable-to-be-outside weather that is incredibly rare in New York. Joseph was coming down from being too high and I was pretty smooshy drunk at that point. We stumbled out and up through the West Village; a few minutes into the walk I stopped in my cowboy boot–trodden tracks. I saw a police horse and I wanted to say hi. The difference between me and most people is that when they come across a police horse, they see a police officer. And me? I see a horse. And that is what white horse-girl privilege will do to you. I walked over and started talking to the officer and asking if I could pet the horse, and asking what kind of horse it was, and blathering on with the confidence that only straightened hair and a liter of rail rum and Diet Coke can bring forth. Meanwhile, Joseph was awkwardly standing by and thinking, *I am way too high to be talking to a cop right now even if that cop is a horse.*

After I finished petting the horse and Joseph realized he wasn't going to be arrested for knowing me, we continued uptown and I reached for his hand. This was my move. Friends don't hold hands. He reluctantly took it and we walked a few more blocks. When we got to the corner of his street, we stopped and I told him that I like liked him. He said, "I'm not a good person to like," and then he kissed me.

We clumsily made it back up to his apartment, passing his shouty doorman, up the stairs, and into his room. This next part I do remember with clarity, as much clarity as something as delicate as memory can allow, but this delicate memory is just for me. I can summarize in a list of adjectives. Clumsy, awkward, sexy, new, hilarious, fun, intimate, amateur, and a good start.

I didn't sleep much. It's always been impossible for me to sleep next to someone after sleeping with them for the first few times; my insecurities, the adrenaline, and my need to always be in control result in a perfect storm of sleeplessness. I learned the cracks and contours of his bedroom ceiling, like I would come to know the cracks and contours of his being.

The next morning, I kissed him goodbye and took myself directly to the CVS Pharmacy, where I got to experience the acute humiliation of having to buy the morning-after pill from a girl I went to high school with. There were two women working behind the counter that day, which was a relief. Regardless of the power dynamic of pharmacy salesclerk/patron, sisterhood is always welcome in times of family planning emergencies. One of the women was being very shouty about customers' orders and prescriptions; there was a long line, and she was working quickly and loudly. I did not want her. I could imagine her hollering, "PLAN B! PLAN B! DO we have any more of the MORNING-AFTER PILL! This chick right HERE needs it!" while pointing to me with my formerly straightened hair now curling from the late-spring humidity and the rolling around on Joseph's bachelor-era unmatched sheets, still donning last night's Slut Suit and the fucking cowboy boots. I did not want her to be my sales representative for this particular purchase. The other salesclerk was the girl I went to high school with. She was a year below me—we were not friends, but I come from a very small town so we definitely had mutual friends and likely worked on a few school plays together. She definitely knew who I was. I remember her as a quiet and clean girl. I was half relieved when she was my clerk.

We made eye contact, I mouthed the words "Plan B," she retrieved a pack and rang me up in total silence. I handed over my $75 and was thankful that it was just one person who knew me who was aware of what I was up to the night before, not the whole CVS full of strangers.

What would you rather? One person who very lightly knows you to know that you were having unprotected sex or the entirety of the Cedar Grove CVS on a Sunday morning? I realized as I wrote this that I could have just gone to another CVS; they are literally fucking everywhere. I chalk it up to being exhausted and the adrenaline from having just leaped over the edge of something big. Joseph still owes me his half of the $75, but at present day I'm willing to forgive that debt as an in-kind contribution to our future.

Earlier that spring I sat next to Joseph on his bed, as it was his only piece of furniture. We were just friends at the time. I felt an odd click in my body the moment my butt touched the bed next to him. It was that strange feeling of intuitive recognition that I had only felt a few times in my life before. It's the feeling of scraping the first layer away of what will become a well-worn groove. When I felt it sitting next to Joseph on his bed it took me by surprise. I was not expecting to feel this in a moment of casually plopping down next to a friend on his sole piece of furniture. I filed the feeling away and waited for life to bring it into focus. This night was when that feeling started to become clearer.

Joseph didn't want a girlfriend. He made that known. He told me, "I'm not a good person to like." But then he kissed me so I was like, "Cool, cool, we'll see about that." He had been in a long-term relationship for years and had recently escaped it. He wanted to be a single guy in NYC, with flings and flirtations. I wanted desperately to be someone's girlfriend, with cuddling and no longer fucking strangers. We were mixing those desires together that night, an alchemy that led to a lot of emotional bruising in the months to come, but on that humid late-spring rum-soaked night those desires were our bottom brick, our basement, our beginning.

2010

Joseph

THIS WAS THE YEAR of settling and settling into. Meg and I had gone from a friendship full of sparks to a summer full of ambiguity, but now we were together for real, although still living in different states. I would head out to New Jersey on weekends, and she would pick me up in her VW Golf that reeked of cigarettes, and on the way to her parents' house where both she and her older sister were still living in the wreckage of the financial crash, we would stop and get pizza from a family-run place called Esposito's. I quickly learned that the best pizza in New York is in New Jersey, which is an open secret that everyone in New Jersey knows and everyone in New York also knows but is in denial about. I liked her parents immediately. Her father is a lawyer who would rather be playing in a bar band, with an abiding love for dogs, gardening, and taking long bike rides while higher than heaven. Her mother is a lawyer who is just fine with being a lawyer, a whip-smart bulldog who relaxes by putting on cable news and shouting profanity at it. Meg and I drank more back then, because our bodies could take it and because what else was there to do on a weekend at your girlfriend's parents' house? We would get high and go hiking with her father and his dogs.

I had come to New York to be a writer, but I mostly spent my days taking customer service calls for the prepaid debit card company. A prepaid debit card is essentially a scam that has paid off enough politicians to be legal, so my job consisted of talking to people who rightly pointed out that we were stealing from them and then I would have to explain, "Yes, but the cops won't do anything about it, sorry." It was, as jobs go, not a rewarding one. I would eat my lunch at my desk while working so I could have my lunch breaks free to walk around Manhattan. For the entire year I took hour-long walks around the city (and sometimes ninety-minute walks—my lunch breaks sprawled on because the company was too small to have anyone watching me closely). I got to know the little parks around the UN and the walking paths along the East River and the strange wasteland of car repair shops and vacant lots near the mistake that is the Javits Center. During those walks I would call my dad, because I didn't know how much time I had left with him, and I would carry his voice around with me as I got to know the island I had moved to. I found myself living for those lunch-break conversations and for the weekends when I would go out to Jersey to be with what was becoming a family for me on the East Coast, because my other family were all a continent away.

Other days I would just go home during my lunch break and take a nap for an hour. I was not a model employee.

Meanwhile, my relationship with my roommate crumbled, and it became clear I needed to escape from Chelsea. In a single afternoon of looking, I found a tiny apartment of my own on Bedford Avenue in Williamsburg, Brooklyn, above a Subway (the chain, not the mode of transportation) and a frozen yogurt store that would go out of business soon after I moved in. The apartment was fine. Sure, the ceiling was coming down a bit, and weird black ooze dripped down the heating pipes, but the owner was a disinterested woman who lived on Long Island, so the rents were absurdly low for a place two blocks from the Bedford L stop.

The week in which I moved was also the biggest blizzard of the year. I didn't have the money for movers. I had to pay down a number of deposits for the new apartment and there was no way I was getting my security back from my grumpy roommate, so I didn't have money for much. I spent almost the entire night in the snow, carting everything I owned down to the subway from Chelsea to Williamsburg, carrying it up to my new place, and then taking the subway back for another load. Then Meg showed up, muscling her Golf through the snowdrifts, to help me carry out the last of it. In my first year of knowing her, Meg helped me move twice. She must have had it bad for me. I don't know what I would have done without her help, although when I mentioned it to her just now, she laughed and said, "I mean, you owned like two things back then."

That junky studio in Williamsburg would become my home for the next four years, and it would be the place where our love grew. Meg would stay the night in my small creaky bed before getting up early to drive all the way out to the insurance office in Secaucus where she worked. We cooked together and ate together and watched TV together, all in bed, because there wasn't really room for any other furniture.

Cara and Chris, friends of ours through the Neo-Futurists, threw loft parties in south Williamsburg. There was fresh cooked food and a lot of drinks and a huge projector screen and a rooftop with weird art projects on it. It was the kind of party that people get invited to in TV shows about Brooklyn, but there we were. "Someday," Meg said to me late one night, in words that carried the sharp smell of booze, "someone is going to write about these parties." And she was, it appears, right about that.

"Let's quit our jobs, so we can just drink beer, write strange stories, wander through bookstores, nap, and eat sausage all day . . ." Meg wrote on my Facebook wall that summer, after a day in Williamsburg where we did just that. I liked Williamsburg. I caught it in the time just after it was too expensive for the artists, but before all the real estate was bought up by foreign investors and the streets were filled with French tourists (for some reason the tourists in Williamsburg are always French. The French are annoyed by Americans, but they also paradoxically set their standards of cool by American pop culture, and so a "cool" American neighborhood is a must-see destination for them). When I moved there, Bedford Avenue was still quiet on weekdays, and the Polish restaurant by the L would still give you good food for cheap. I would walk down to the waterfront in the evening after work. The waterfront has a perfect view of the Williamsburg Bridge, which is the prettiest bridge in New York City despite the Brooklyn Bridge getting all the attention. From that vantage you could watch the planes come in for landing at all three of the city's airports as the sun set over Manhattan. For someone who, along with a new pounding anxiety, had developed a serious fear of flying, it was a comforting place to stand and talk on the phone to the people I missed: Meg during the week, my dad on weekends.

On one of those calls, Meg told me that a squirrel had sequestered itself behind her front door and she was trying to figure out how to get the squirrel to leave. With me on the phone, she moved the door a little, and the squirrel took the opportunity to jump out at her face. She screamed, and the squirrel ran away.

"I have to deal with this. Talk to you later. Love you," she said. And then she hung up.

Seconds later, she texted. "I may have just said I love you. I do." Then she texted, "Awkward squirrel."

I texted back, "I love you too."

We were true millennials, expressing our love for the first time by text. If there had been an app we could have downloaded to do it, we might have done that instead.

Our identities as lovers were wrapped up in our identities as artists. She was working toward becoming a member of the New York Neo-Futurists. She was so focused on it that for the first several months of our relationship, she insisted we keep the two of us secret. Her worry was that, since we were both peripherally involved in the company, our relationship might hurt her chances even a little to be cast. We abided by that, as obvious as I think our relationship was to the outside world, until we were having a lunch with a number of our friends, including several Neo-Futurists, and Meg mentioned she had once given a blow job just after eating several very hot peppers.

"Good lord," one of them asked. "How was it for him?"

"I don't know," she said. "You can ask him." And pointed to me.

We hadn't discussed going public. All the faces turned to look at me. I was about to bite into my hamburger. I set it back down on my plate and folded my hands.

"It hurt," I said.

While Meg tried to become a Neo-Futurist, I tried to become the person I had always imagined myself being, even as I wasn't clear who that person was. I gradually added, one by one, to the cemetery of unfinished novels that was my laptop's writing folder (carefully copied from computer to computer so faithfully that there are, as of this writing, files in there with Last Modified dates in the 1990s; short stories written in elementary school; class assignments from seventh grade; my bar mitzvah speech). I also vaguely wanted to be a musician like my father, and so I did a few open-mic nights and wrote songs. It all felt half-hearted, because that's what it was. I decided I just needed to follow a project through, no matter what it was.

The first of these projects was a book of short stories written by all of my writer friends that I commissioned, edited, and then laid out myself in free software that came with my computer. The software was designed to allow people to make their own greeting cards at home. There were no templates, so I laid out each of the 300 or so pages of the book individually. Then I called around to printers for quotes, printed a few hundred copies, and convinced a couple of local bookstores to carry it. We had a launch party at the late Bar 82 in the East Village, a lousy bar that had a great back room they would rent out to artists for a hundred bucks, including a sound person for the night. Meg and the rest of the writers in the book did readings. There were musicians. A friend of ours brought cupcakes themed around the book. I had finished something. It felt amazing. We went out to find that Meg's car had been towed, and spent much of the rest of the night at the impound on the West Side Highway, where finally Meg signed her name in a leather-bound register that looked to be a hundred years old, and was given back her Volkswagen.

The other project I completed that year was a birthday gift for Meg. She wanted to perform in downtown New York theater, and I wanted to write downtown New York theater, so I wrote her a play and got it placed in a small festival that summer at the Theater for the New City on Second Avenue. The play was about us and about my anxiety. It was our relationship from her point of view, as written by me, and the weirdness of that appealed to both of us. I also chose to direct it, which led to a lot of fighting. It was the first of many things we worked on together, and we hadn't yet learned to trust each other's instincts. We performed the show in the festival three times, to a crowd mostly of friends. Meg had total commitment to the play, throwing her body around during one section so roughly that she still credits those performances with her bad back. I sat in the dark booth, running sound cues off a CD I had burned, and watching this woman I loved perform the hell out of her first solo work in New York City, and my first script of any kind ever produced. It was the start of learning how each other worked and was in retrospect practice for all of the other stuff we'd go on to build together: theater, podcasts, homes, a life.

Early that summer, a few weeks before our show, we took a trip to California with my family, our first real trip together. We flew to Los Angeles, rented a car, and began the drive up the coast. I drove us along the 101 up past Santa Barbara, then cutting out to the 1 at San Luis Obispo and arriving finally at Cambria, a beautiful town of redwoods and tide pools twenty minutes down the coast from Hearst

Castle, the house of the newspaper tycoon and a gaudy monument to the necessity for massive taxes on the rich.

It is hard to recapture for myself what it felt like to take this vacation. We both worked low-paying office jobs in the ruins of what the financial collapse had left us, but we splurged as far as our budget would take us, staying at a bed-and-breakfast in town that had a free wine mixer at 5 P.M. every day (!) and going to dinner at a place called Robin's that was just across the street. Robin's is quintessential coastal Californian, set in a fragrant herb garden and serving everything from simple roast chicken to Indonesian satay to Indian curries. Meg and I ordered a flight of local wines and they came as three full glasses, so in my memory Cambria dances. The lights of the town are drunk too, and they stumble with us. The next day, we drove up the coast to see elephant seals the size of minivans fight and grumble and huddle for warmth.

Then farther up the coast, a stop in Monterey for the aquarium and a stop in San Francisco to see it before the billionaires murdered it, and then we were up in Point Reyes. My family had rented a house. It was one of the last times we were together as an entire family before my father died, and although none of us knew that, we all suspected it could be true. There was no surprise to my father's death, but also no certainty. We knew it would happen soon, but we didn't know when, and so every time could be the last time. We hiked and cooked dinner together and did sing-alongs of Van Morrison to my father's piano playing. Meg performed the one-woman show in the living room, carefully leaving out the part about us having sex.

2010 was the first year that we woke up as a couple on New Year's Day. Snowed in at a Marriott in Boston, where we had gone to see some of Meg's college friends and celebrate at a bar where the New Year's last call had been at 11:30 P.M. The next morning Meg was still in the spandex bodysuit that she wore at all times during this period and said to me sleepily, "I'm still in my catsuit." It was the first year we lived as a couple, with all the awkward choreography that kind of thing involves until the edges of each life can be smoothed down to fit comfortably together. We didn't know who we were as a couple yet because we didn't know who we were as people yet. We were asking a lot of ourselves, and we hadn't learned any of the answers. It was the year of settling and settling into. And so, we gladly did.

Meg

IN DECEMBER OF 2009, after months of casually dating with serious feelings, Joseph gave in to my wants and asked to be together exclusively. I had made out with a random in a bar in Rhode Island on Thanksgiving weekend 2009. Upon my return, when I casually mentioned it in conversation, Joseph was shocked. I was like, "You've never called me your girlfriend, so I macked it to a punk dude who thought I was the coolest thing since menthol cigarettes. If you want me to not do that, then you know what to call me." I think that pushed him over the edge from wanting a casual thing to wanting a real thing.

Now we were a real thing complete with New Year's plans and regular sleepovers, but I found myself tentative, like walking on newly frozen ice. I snared my prey but I was reluctant to consume it. This sort of "real thing" relationship was a new world to me, and when I entered this new world, I brought my old self with me, an old self with a lot of protective layers. I needed to know if he was with me because he liked being with me or only with me because my tricks and traps of homemade meatballs and blow jobs had worked. That's sometimes the thing with wanting something very badly, getting it, and then not being sure you deserve it. It's the shrapnel wounds from the ongoing blasts of deep-set self-hatred that fans out into every aspect of who you are.

I used to be a binge eater. I actually still am but it's something I've learned to manage. It's like your hometown: even after you move away you will have always once lived there. You will always be from there. It will always be a fact of your existence. As a kid, I would come home from school every day and empty the contents of the fridge and pantry into my body. I would think of nothing and feel no pain while I was bingeing, and then I would feel ill and ashamed. And then I would binge more. All of the cruelty and criticisms heaped on me by my peers and by the adults in my life because I was a chubby kid caused an ingrained self-hatred. For me it was cyclical. I was a fat kid. I took abuse for that existence. I binge ate to soothe the pain. It made me larger. I was a child who was learning to deal with the complex emotions of being a fat human in this fat-hating world years before the words "body positivity" had been uttered by a single influencer, and my outlet was self-harm.

I'm still the same person as I was when I was a bullied, hurt kid, but I did stop binge eating. I found new ways to numb, to harm, some that made me lose a lot of weight. Losing weight made all of the people who hated my fat body cheer for me even though I was just as sick as before. But it was easier. It is easier to navigate this world in a less fat body. I've been the heads and the tails of that coin, and I hate the fact of it, but it's true. I saw just how much disgust and hatred was hurled at me by my society when I was able to use my thin privilege to step out of the line of fire. The comments that were usually reserved for behind my back were said to my face, directed to some other person who I used to look a lot like. This experience is inextricable from my understanding of my own self-worth and self-love. Understanding how to be loved by someone when you don't love yourself and have been made to believe you are undeserving of love is a complicated emotional process that I began to navigate with Joseph.

From 2004 to 2010 I smoked weed every single day of my life. No matter the weather, no matter the location. As a pattern, I replaced one self-destructive behavior with another. Instead of food going in, it was smoke and powder (so much lighter!). I smoked a pack or more of Camels a day and would recreationally use cocaine and Vicodin whenever the party allowed. This provided the same numbness from self-hatred that I had grown addicted to but with way more social interaction. It's much more fun to party all night and day with friends than it is to eat an entire loaf of whole wheat bread and then throw up.

In 2010, I gradually and almost imperceptibly stopped smoking weed and doing party drugs. I replaced one thing with another again. This time it wasn't one self-destructive behavior for the other, but the filling of that seemingly unfillable space with actual . . . fulfillment. I began forming a life that pulled me *into* the world instead of away from the pain of it. I had the beginnings of a creative identity. And I had a person who liked having me around, who made me feel seen and understood. I slowly started to peel back the layers of self-hatred and began to see myself as a person deserving of love.

I made it through my intern year with the Neo-Futurists and began working for them as a technical collaborator and as a production manager/dramaturge for one of their mainstage shows, called *The Soup Show*. The premise of *The Soup Show* was three naked women in a hot tub talking about feminism and women's bodies in our society. It was a new work, and I got to be involved in the process of building the show with an incredible team of women. This show was a huge step forward artistically for me. The previous year, I was washing ball sweat out of dance costumes for less than minimum wage. Now I was producing new feminist experimental theater for less than minimum wage.

A normal day for me would be my 9-to-5 job at an insurance agency in Jersey followed by a commute to Brooklyn for an evening rehearsal of *The Soup Show*, then a quick drive back over the Williamsburg Bridge just before midnight to Joseph's apartment in Chelsea, where we would talk about our big days in his little rented bed while dozing off. Then I would get up in the morning, carefully try to avoid running into his weird roommate, grab a coffee at the corner, and drive back to Jersey for another round of the learning-to-be-a-working-artist hustle complete with the soul-sucking customer service day job bonus pack. The schedule was equally draining and invigorating. My days were the fullest they had ever been. It felt great to have a partner who was equally as passionate as me about building our artistic foundations.

Eventually Joseph's terrible roommate caught on to the fact that I was sleeping there most nights and not paying rent. We talked with him about us paying more and me moving in, but we were not ready to move in together. Our relationship was new, and we were young. We were both way more focused on hustling our careers forward than sharing in domestic bliss. This waffling on me moving in ultimately led to Joseph's terrible roommate insinuating that I was a sex worker and Joseph moving out, marking the second time I would help him move in my very small Volkswagen.

In March of 2010 Joseph moved into an apartment on Bedford Avenue in Williamsburg, Brooklyn. Which was a 1 bed/0.5 bath/0.5 bath (yeah that's a possible configuration, who fucking knew?) above a Subway restaurant and soon-to-be-defunct frozen yogurt shop that would ultimately become a nail salon. Please take a moment to imagine the combined smell of nail salon and Subway sandwich. Really think about the scent notes of plasticized industrial bread making and methyl methacrylate violently dancing together in your olfactory bulbs; breathe deep, friends, this was our life. Also, the entrance vestibule to the building was a popular urinal for local homeless people.

While the apartment smelled weird and bizarrely had a small carpeted room containing a toilet and then another room on the other side of the apartment containing a sink and shower, it was our up-and-coming artist hipster kid clubhouse and we loved it. It was one train stop from the Neo-Futurists theater in the East Village, so we could stay out real late after weekend shows, drinking whiskeys and having deep artistic conversations about the theatrical value of onstage queefing and laughing our cheeks off at jokes about death and depression with our community of artists and drinkers. Then we would sleep in the next morning and stumble to the bagel shop, hand in hand. It was a pretty good time. I'm romanticizing it now, but it was very romantic then, in the way that being broke struggling young artists in love will always be, as trite as it is completely unique.

During the course of this year there were hundreds of times when I wanted to tell Joseph I loved him. I was a frequent user of the L word. I always said it to my parents, sister, and close friends when saying goodbye. In 2007, one of my roommates from college was killed in a car crash. My last conversation with her was over the phone, and I ended it with my standard "Love ya, bye!" It brought me comfort in the process of mourning her to know that was the last thing I said to her. I want that to be the last thing I say to everyone I love. So, it was weird that I hadn't said it to Joseph yet. I think up until this point I had managed an "I'm very fond of you." It always felt weird leaving him and being like, "I know we are incredibly close but I'm too afraid of showing you how I feel because I fear rejection so acutely that I am paralyzed so, uhh, later, braaaah."

There are different rules with saying "I love you" to a romantic partner. It's pulling the curtain back and hoping that everything behind it is enough. The stakes are ratcheted up. It breaks your character of being cool and aloof. It bars your ability to move on with your shell intact, if he were to not feel the same. It's leaping without a net. But the day I leapt came without intention. I had just gotten home to New Jersey from work on an early spring day and I was on the phone with Joseph. He was telling me that he wasn't feeling well. Being a California kid he never had to deal with East Coast seasonal allergies before. He was a tender, tender child. While I was on the phone with him, I went outside to check the mail, and when I got to the mailbox there was a squirrel trapped behind the shutter that the mailbox was mounted to. I freaked out and began trying to free the squirrel, with Joseph still on the phone. I abruptly said, "I gotta go, I hope you feel better, I love you very much." CLICK. I pulled the shutter back and the squirrel ran off and I realized what I had just done. I texted Joseph immediately being like, "Uhhh, the squirrel made me say it . . ."

He texted back "I feel that way too."

So that is what it took to break down my defenses, to push me over the edge, a trapped squirrel and a cute boy with a runny nose.

While we were taking that very definitive next step out loud, an even more meaningful step was happening quietly. Not to be all early-aughts boy in a hat singer/songwriter, but love is a verb. It's an action. It's not something inert that sits on a shelf, it is something you do that creates an effect. That year for his birthday, I bought him a wok from Amazon. For my birthday, he wrote a one-woman show for me to star in and got it produced in a new-work festival at Theater for the New City. He won the gifting that year. He verbed me. He verbed me good.

The play was called *Pro-Life*, and it had nothing to do with abortion, but its name made it so I could never put it on my resume and so we would always have to say, "It's not about abortion!" when telling people about it. He wrote it and I performed it and we directed it together. He didn't come from a theater background, and I had an expensive piece of paper that said I was a Big Deal Bachelor of the make-pretend Arts. I lived on my high horse during the rehearsal process so much so that I'm surprised I didn't get saddle sores. We brought in two outside directors who we both trusted to help us: Erica Livingston, who was a fellow Neo-Futurist and would go on to be the voice of Alice in Joseph's podcast *Alice Isn't Dead*, and Jeffrey Cranor, another Neo-Futurist, who would go on to be Joseph's writing and business partner on *Welcome to Night Vale*. The two of them helped us stage and bring shape to the piece and served as a buffer for us fighting over who got to call the shots. They were helpful stewards for the two of us learning to collaborate together.

We were ultimately very proud of that piece. My favorite section to perform was the end, where I slipped and fell on a banana peel over and over until it stopped being funny. It started as a clown bit with big lead-ups and funny faces, and it ended with me repeatedly slamming my body into the ground. The audience laughed a lot at the beginning and ended with them gasping, my favorite type of theater to make. My back will never recover, but it was worth it. It was Joseph's and my first large-scale collaboration, and we 1) made a good piece of art, 2) began learning how to trust each other's artistic choices, and 3) worked on something challenging together and enjoyed it.

Making work together would become an important piece of our relationship. Another huge piece of our relationship would be traveling together. This summer marked our first big trip together to California. We had spent weekends away here and there, but this trip would be much larger scale. It was a two-part trip, the first being a road trip for the two of us, and the second being a week with his family in the country.

We flew to LA and drove up the Pacific coast highway to Point Reyes, stopping in Cambria for the night. I brought my blue tie-dyed Snuggie* for the plane, and Joseph, rightfully, pretended not to know me. I also went to Marshalls before the trip and spent $19.99 on some very cheaply assembled lingerie for our night at a fancy bed-and-breakfast I rented in Cambria. He remembered he knew me then. He referred to it as my "hotel suit" for years.

Joseph's dad rented the car for us because at that point we were too young to rent one on our own. I was salty when I realized I couldn't smoke in the car. A road trip without smoking was a very foreign concept to me, as foreign a concept to me as suddenly having a boyfriend with whom I created plays and went on romantic drives up the California coast. In one of my previous relationships, a "romantic date" consisted of going to the combination KFC/Taco Bell after I drove him to DUI court. I was a stranger in a strange land, and this land had

---

* When I think back to how I used to pack, I shudder. Years of touring really teach you about essentials. A Snuggie is bullshit. It is something an amateur would bring on a trip. I was an amateur.

beaches with tide pools, grumpy elephant seals, dinner in a lush garden, and not a single greasy bag of cold popcorn chicken or municipal court magistrate in sight. It was a good kind of strange, worth trading constant access to nicotine for.

I never had a boyfriend who wanted to introduce me to his family. I never thought I would have that, that I was deserving of that. Before Joseph, I was the after-dark girl, the casual thing, the let's-keep-this-between-us person. I expected him to be embarrassed by me and my big thighs and loud mouth, but he wasn't. He didn't see me that way, the way I had learned to see myself. I felt like a character in a mistaken-identity farce, suddenly waking up in someone else's life and trying like hell not to be made for who I really was.

A theme in my life has always been, whenever I get one of those moments, those dream-come-true, can't-believe-this-is-your-real-life moments, I'm knocked back down to earth, usually literally. That moment happened on the Santa Monica Pier. I tripped over my flip-flopped feet and stubbed my toe. I caught a few splinters, a small scrape, and was moderately bleeding. It was not a big deal until we went to stop at Joseph's aunt and uncle's house in Shell Beach so I could meet them. My toe was still actively bleeding when I walked into their stunning beach house with light-colored carpeting. They were very welcoming and I did my best to make a good impression and have that impression not be a trail of blood.

We arrived in Point Reyes to meet up with his parents, sister, and brother-in-law. Joseph's family was very warm and accepting. They were all very smart and musically talented. I'm smart but not musically talented, but his dad was able to wear me down to sing a Carole King song late in the trip. We spent the week hiking, relaxing, spending family time, and rehearsing for *Pro-Life* whenever possible. You learn a lot about a person by getting to know their family. Up until this trip I was very conscious of the ways Joseph was slowly changing me, encouraging my creative focus, breaking down my walls of needing to be cool, slowly weaning me off of my vices of cigarettes, rage, and hard drugs, inspiring feelings of self-love and confidence in myself. I hadn't noticed the ways I had been changing him until I saw him with his family. You could see the buds of us growing into our own family. It was subtle, but there, he was more forthcoming with his feelings, more conscious of other people's feelings; he was becoming more organized, and he was eating more cheese, all things that were definitely my influence.

Toward the end of the trip, we went two-person kayaking on Tomales Bay, the ultimate test of a new relationship, wherein we were forced to work together to avoid crashing into a splintery dock or capsizing the kayak containing Joseph's lovely parents. Wherein I had to size up my body and admit to myself and to everyone at Kayak Struggle Adventures™ or whatever the fuck the boat rental place was called that my boyfriend weighed less than me and therefore I needed to sit in the back of the kayak, and I needed to try not to spend the rest of the day (or my life) hating myself because of that. I got in the back of the boat and he still loved me. I felt like I had been exhaustively striving to hide the most obvious part of myself, and now I knew everyone could see it and IT DIDN'T MATTER ONE GD BIT. No matter what the world had told me about my body—that I was unlovable, unfuckable, and that I should hate myself for taking up more space—it wasn't true. Women can weigh more than the men who love them! It had been proved false by the simple act of getting in a shitty plastic boat.

I wish I could say that I didn't need anyone else's approval to love myself, but for me that's not true. I needed someone to love me for who I was and not for what I looked like in order for me to believe that I was worthy of love and that I could be of value in a relationship. I will always be from a hometown of self-hate and destruction, but I don't have to visit all the time. I have better places to visit, and I have a two-person kayak to help row.

Joseph and I found ourselves in a boat with a singular mission but dueling leadership. It took us a good bit to get over our shit and work together, but when we found a rhythm, we really sliced across the water and could see just how beautiful that big blue bay is. We didn't know then how much we would need those skills of working together to stay above water while enjoying the view. I'm thankful every day for the water splashed on our young faces by kayak paddles. Paddles that narrowly missed our skulls and found their way into the water and back out again coating us in salt. Salt that worked its way into us and made us who we would need to be for what was coming next.

2011

Joseph

THIS ONE ISN'T EASY to write, just as it was not easy to live.

In early summer of 2011, my father, having struggled for years with a failing heart, went in for a procedure called an ablation, where the parts of the heart causing abnormal electrical signals are cauterized. As soon as they put him under anesthesia, his heart stopped. His surgery was in Santa Barbara, but his condition upon restarting his heart became so bad that they drove him the two hours down to Los Angeles, to the Cedars-Sinai intensive care. The head cardiologist of the hospital said he needed to be put on the transplant list that night. But the transplant program administrator insisted on going through three days of paperwork before she would let that happen, saying that doctors always think everything they do is so important and not to worry. While the paperwork was slowly filed, a viable heart came in, and went to someone else, because my dad was not yet on the list. The doctors were furious when they heard, but the administrator continued plodding on with the paperwork. The American medical system, as I'm sure you don't need reminding, is inhumane and broken.

I flew out from New York to be with my dad and my family. Meg wasn't with me. This was also the year that the dream she had been striving for over three years finally happened. She had started working to be a member of the New York Neo-Futurists in late 2008. Three years later, she was finally given the opportunity to audition. She put together a piece in which she cut off her hair, hair that she hadn't cut in five years. Her commitment was absolute. And it paid off. They accepted her. (Which, of course. They were lucky to have her. She could write, and perform, but also, she could organize and fix problems. In a community of artists, one organized person is more valuable than a thousand creative geniuses.) She would finally step into the show we had been watching together for all these years and perform in it. The week of her first show was the week my dad ended up in intensive care. I told her it was fine. He wasn't going anywhere yet, and she had worked so hard. So, while I sat long days in the uncomfortable chairs of the Cedars-Sinai intensive care unit waiting room, Meg achieved her dreams. I was sad she wasn't with me. I was sad that this moment of deserved triumph for her was being countered by the relentless cruelty of life. I was just sad. I was fucking sad.

The windows of the ICU waiting room looked out at the Largo, a theater that would later become a regular stop for Meg's and my touring live show, although of course we did not know that then.

My mom and I would drive out from Camarillo, an hour and a half away, early in the morning, joining rush hour, which is mostly a lot of people getting frustrated about not going fast enough to a place they don't want to be. For us I suppose it was more complicated. Obviously, we didn't want to go to a hospital and watch a person we loved suffer through a failing heart. But we wanted to be by his side. I remember the hours in the car. Back and forth. Back and forth. We listened to podcasts. We talked. It's mundane, the worst moments of your life. They're made of the same fabric as the rest of it. It feels like there should be fanfare. I remember us talking about the retirement of the space shuttle, which was happening that month. My mother always had a passion for space. A lot of things were ending that month, I suppose. I suppose a lot of things I'll never hear about started too. It was just a normal month, then, for everyone but us.

We would get there and go see my father when we could. It was a cardiac intensive care unit, so someone was always dying. The shriek of alarms for a coding patient was a constant background noise, reminding every other patient what could happen next to any of them.

This is where I'm supposed to say my father looked small or strange or not himself, with the tubes and wires and monitors winding around him. But it was worse than that. He looked just like himself, but he couldn't get up. He couldn't walk out of there with us. He was having nightmares, he told us. In his dreams he would go for a run, as he had done every single day of his life until his heart condition forced him to stop, and then he would fall and badly hurt himself. It felt strange, that dreaming was possible in that place. But our brain can take us away from anywhere. His window had a perfect view of the Hollywood sign, which he couldn't see, because his bed faced away from it. We sang songs together. As a family we had always sung songs together. We were only ourselves in that room, as we had always been, but everything else was wrong. They still wouldn't put him on the transplant list yet because he had gotten an infection, we were told. Some men came by who had gotten heart transplants to talk about what life was like afterward. My father and my mother finally considered, for the first time since my father had learned his heart was failing seven years earlier, what old age might look like for the two of them. The infection lingered, but once it had cleared, he was first in line for a transplant. We hoped that as soon as it did, some young healthy person with a future in front of them would die in a car crash so that my father could live. That's what it is to wait for a heart transplant. Love turns you into a vulture. I couldn't stay longer than a week. I had already taken off so much work. My father was stable. I flew home.

My flight was on a Friday afternoon. The airline was Continental, which ceased to exist less than a year later. Everything ends. That Saturday I saw Meg in the show, amazed at the way she had gotten herself where she had long wanted to be. People came up to me, spoke in hushed and concerned tones, and as is often the case when you are in pain, I mostly reassured them rather than the other way around. Yes, he's ok. It's not great, but he'll get a transplant soon. I'm expecting a call any minute now, night or day, letting me know that we have a heart for him. We went out drinking to celebrate at Stillwater, the Oklahoma-themed dive bar across the street from the theater, a regular after-show stop because it was cheap and the tables in the back were always empty. The week I am writing these words, Stillwater is finally going out of business. Everything ends. As the sun rose, Meg and I settled on my sagging mattress on the floor of my shitty apartment. This was before Meg moved in, so the mattress was still oriented between the two windows, not yet moved onto a bed frame facing the TV. I remember exactly where it was, because I remember exactly where I was sitting when I woke up, grabbed my phone from off the TV stand, and saw I had a missed call from my mother, and a voicemail. I felt a surge of excitement and fear. He had finally gotten the heart. My father was probably already in surgery. I listened to the message. My father had died the night before, as Meg and I slept off her first weekend in the show. Neither my sister nor my mother had been with him. After all the time we spent around his bed, he died surrounded by strangers. I think it was the infection he got in the hospital, the one that kept him off the transplant list, but I don't know that for sure. I never asked. I remember the floating feeling. I remember Meg's hand on my back as she realized what was happening. I called JetBlue, got last-minute tickets for the next day. Jews bury their dead quickly. Meg came with me this time, missing her second weekend in the show she had worked years to get into. What shit timing life has.

My father's favorite song was "The Water Is Wide," so I sang it at his funeral, a cappella, on the same bimah I had gotten bar mitz-vahed on. There is a verse about love fading and growing cold, and my mother asked me to rewrite that, because it didn't describe her and my father's loving relationship. So I rewrote it as the following, using the images of my father's garden he had gone out to tend every single day, and the coastline that we had hiked together all through my childhood:

The overgrown lavender, and the perfumed rose
Love lasts longer, much longer than those
Pebbled beaches, chaparral-crowned bluffs
Love lasts longer than any of us

We buried him in the Jewish cemetery in Ventura. You could smell the ocean a little, just a little, from his grave. Meg and I flew home a couple of days later. We both had to get back to work. Life doesn't stop, even when it stops.

That was the year of Occupy Wall Street, when the feeling that had bubbled since the financial collapse, the deep feeling that nothing was right and that the gamblers of Wall Street were to blame, that feeling finally pushed people to take to the streets. I didn't go down to the park or attend any meetings. I was too busy trying to get a writing career started in between working at a predatory financial services company to go protest predatory financial services companies. But I was there for the big march. I joined the tens of thousands. The police lined the route, decked out in their military dress-up, like they were soldiers in a righteous and glorious war rather than overpaid bullies out intimidating kids. "I don't see no riot here," the crowd chanted at them, "so why'd you bring your riot gear?" I was still in so much pain from my father's death. I marched close to the cops, almost wishing one of them would hit me. Of course, they're not interested in beating people who look like me. A month later the NYPD crushed Occupy Wall Street for good, making New York safe again for the wealthy investors who buy all the apartments but never live in them.

A month after my father died, my mother's dog died. The dog couldn't walk. My mom had to carry this large dog to the car, drive her to the shelter, and ask them to put the dog out of her misery. My mom didn't call any of us for help. But then, I was across the country, what could I have done?

At my job at the prepaid debit card company, the elevator started acting strangely. It would open three feet below the chosen floor, and the passengers would have to step up to get out. It would jerk violently mid-operation. I didn't trust it. We were on the sixth floor, so I started taking the stairs. One day, sitting at my desk, I heard a bang. The elevator had fallen from our floor to the basement. The passenger had broken his leg. I knew that my time at that job was coming to a close. I had spent almost three years at that desk, waiting for something else to happen. I felt that the wait was almost over, although I couldn't imagine what was next.

Meanwhile my sister had been planning her wedding, which had been scheduled to take place that year. At first, she canceled it after my father's death. Then she decided to move forward with it. Life doesn't stop, even when it stops. I was frayed to the end of it. My anxiety, a creature running loose inside of me since that summer in 2009, had fully taken over after my father's death. And it focused on flying. I was petrified of flying. Already I had flown to and from California twice in a week, once to be with my father as he died, once to be at his funeral. I couldn't take another flight so soon. The thought ate me up inside. I couldn't sleep. I told my sister that all the moving of dates around meant I didn't know if I could come. This was an excuse, because I didn't know how to explain that the thought of getting on a plane one more time seemed like it would literally cause me to die. That merely stepping one foot on that plane would be what killed me. My sister was hurt, of course, and of course we did finally go. The entire flight, I rewatched old sitcom episodes that I'd watched a million times, letting the stale jokes carry me through my nightmare. Meg, as she would for countless flights after, held my hand during takeoff.

And I haven't even mentioned yet (an eventful year for sure) that this was the year I first started writing with Jeffrey, who would go on to be my co-writer on *Welcome to Night Vale* and all that came after that. He had suggested we write a play together, and so all through that year we had been meeting, writing a play about time travel and regret called *What the Time Traveler Will Tell Us*. We secured a space to perform it in the Incubator Arts Space in St. Mark's Church, a space that had served as a venue for experimental theater for decades. Two years after we performed there, the venue shut down and the space reopened as a ballet school. Everything ends. The play was set to debut in early August. A month earlier, all this happened. I did the play anyway. I was miserable and frustrated and grumpy. The play was strange and abstract. My co-workers from the prepaid debit card company came one night, which was really very sweet, and they mumbled that it was interesting. Jeffrey and I shared a love for podcasts, and I started thinking maybe we should make a podcast together. This idea settled in the back of my mind.

My sister got married in a park in Topanga at sunset. It smelled of flowers and herbs. There were photos of my father in the reception hall. We made do with what was left of us, our family. Four years later, Meg and I would celebrate our wedding in the same park, but we didn't know that yet. My sister would have a son, and then another son. We didn't know any of that. After her second son, her heart too would fail, postpartum cardiomyopathy, and we would once again be in intensive care. This time the story would end differently. My sister would walk out of the hospital alive. But we didn't know any of that. The evening of her wedding there was only dancing and the signing of the ketubah as the white-winged moths flitted in and out of the lamplight. It smelled like lavender and sage, the wind coming off the chaparral. The same chaparral that I had recently sung about at my father's funeral. As I write these words, my sister's oldest son is seven. He knows all about his grandpa, although the two can never meet.

That New Year's Eve was a quiet one. We stayed in, at my tiny apartment in Williamsburg. Meg made lentil soup. I made rosemary raisin bread. I had been sick for a couple weeks, 2011 leaving the last of its claws in me as it departed. There hasn't been a worse year yet, but I don't doubt one is coming. Some year has got to be your worse one. Without the bad years, the good years may not seem so sweet.

But I don't want to end this year on New Year's, because that wasn't the important bit. Dates and holidays are arbitrary. Our lives are shaped by darker and wilder stuff. I want to end this year back in July, only a few days after my father died. Meg and I were in my childhood bedroom. I don't know if it was the day of the funeral or the day before or the day after. Those days sunk into each other, and I can't separate them easily in my memory. But this moment is clear. We're lying in bed. It's the middle of the day. We're taking a nap I think, except we're both awake. We're lying on our sides.

"I could spend the rest of my life with you," I said.

"That'd be nice," she said.

Neither of us said anything more for a while. It was the first time that the possibility of forever was presented to us, just days after the reality of how these things end was brutally demonstrated. We wouldn't get married for another few years, but my assumption from then on was that our relationship was a lifelong one. That moment was when the scope of what we were building together was made clear to me. And I guess that moment, along with many other moments, is the important bit.

Meg

WHEN CATALOGING MEMORY, I often think about what I wore. I think a lot of people do this. It makes sense that the things that help us remember are the things that are physically closest to our bodies. Girdle, blue socks, leg warmers, tap shoes, pink nightdress, sensible black dress—these are the things I remember wearing in 2011. Not all at once, of course; that would be ridiculous.

I've had a complicated relationship with clothing for most of my life. I've had a complicated relationship with my body for most of my life. These things go hand in glove. I don't think I have consistently worn the same size of clothing for more than three years of my life ever. I've ranged from a size 26 to a size 6. I wake up every morning with a slightly different body, a brand-new assignment of who I am, every day. It's difficult to clothe a body that does not fit into the standard definition of normal. You can't shop at the "normal" stores, you can't borrow your friend's or your sister's clothes. You have to try on thirty pairs of jeans to maybe find one that isn't horrible (goddamn the early-aughts trend of low-cut jeans, goddamn that shit to a hell made entirely of ass cracks). Clothing is tough. Clothing is exhausting. Clothing is memory. Clothing is identity. Clothing is required. Clothing is something I use to try to control the out-of-control relationship I have with my body, and frankly, that's a lot of pressure to put on a T-shirt.

In the spring of 2011, Joseph and I both auditioned for the New York Neo-Futurists. Only I was called back. Being a Neo-Futurist became less of a priority for Joseph than it was when we first got together. His foot had eased off the gas of obsession, mine had not. My sole focus for the past three years was to be cast as a New York Neo-Futurist. Every choice I made was in an effort to achieve that one goal. Joseph put on a brave face for me, because the rejection of not being called back stung for him, but he didn't let this sting enter our world. He made me feel assured, confident, and supported during the auditions and callbacks. He helped me edit my pieces. He watched me practice tap dancing in his tiny kitchen. He ate burritos with me. Sometimes you just need someone to eat a burrito with you. My mind was constantly ticking through ideas for pieces and going over my monologues. There was room for nothing else in my one-track mind. He made sure I didn't career off the road of the living from the distractions of these ridiculous auditions.

Auditioning for anything is a lesson in emotional vulnerability. Auditioning for the Neo-Futurists is a master's degree in emotional vulnerability. The auditions and callbacks are a multiweek process, culminating in a two-day-long workshop with the full ensemble and all of the fellow auditionees. Throughout the process you are required to present five to ten short pieces of new work based on your life and current events. The work must be completely honest, evocative, and dynamic enough to separate you from the pack of the other auditionees. You have to go big. For my initial audition, I wore only a ridiculous one-piece girdle that went from midthigh to my armpits and I shotgunned a SlimFast while talking about the diet culture I was raised in. For my callback pieces, I put on my tap shoes from when I was in the chorus of my middle school's production of *Dames at Sea* in seventh grade and I furiously tap danced to the best of my nonexistent capabilities while delivering a monologue about Gilda Radner and who gets to decide what "good" art is. For my final piece I tasked a fellow auditionee to cut off a foot of my long hair while I performed a monologue about losing people, leaving things behind, and growing up. In addition to our prepared pieces, we were tasked with creating new work on the fly, being given ten or fifteen minutes to create a new play from various prompts. We also were to perform in our fellow auditionees' pieces. And, of course, there was a full job interview, where you sat in a hot seat and were interviewed by the ensemble of eighteen people and tried to sound as smart and capable as your exhausted and bedraggled self could sound. Being able to go back to Joseph's apartment after running that emotional and physical gamut, and feel like no matter what happened he would still love me, was the quiet cool pillow that my hot tired head needed more than anything.

I was sitting on my couch in my parents' house with my newly minted haircut when I got the phone call that I was cast. I felt like I had climbed a mountain and not only had I reached the top, I belonged there. I fit. I knew that I was good enough; I spent the past three years learning everything I could about this form of theater to make damn sure I would be. But I still didn't know that I would get it. I was the best at things before, and that had not mattered. I was given the "she's gotta stand in the back because she doesn't look like the other girls" so many times before. It felt amazing to get to stand in the front this time. I never had any doubt that I belonged on that stage and, for once in my life, nobody else did, either.

Now that I had been cast as a Neo-Futurist, I began preparing for my first run of performances. I grappled with what I was going to wear onstage. As a Neo-Futurist, you don't play a character. You are always yourself onstage. You tell your stories. You do real tasks and you wear your own clothes, no costumes, no fourth wall. You are always you. The show is very physical and messy. Most of the ensemble wears jeans or shorts, some form of pants. If I were to wear pants onstage, the moment I bent over to pick something up two-thirds of my ass crack would be on display. I have a very long ass. My ass crack starts midback and goes all the way to my knees. Pants are not designed to fit my body. For my first show I decided on leggings, with leg warmers to balance out the width of my thighs and a skirt with pockets.* The skirt would serve as an ass cover and the pockets were helpful to hold small props. I picked out blue ankle socks because they reminded me of Dorothy from *The Wizard of Oz*. She wore blue socks with her ruby slippers; there was power in that. I wouldn't be dressed like anyone else onstage but that was ok. I didn't need to be like anyone else. They cast me because they needed me, not a version of me trying to wear skinny jeans like the skinny girls.

Right as I was to start my first week performing with the Neo-Futurists, we received the news that Joseph's dad, Ron, was very sick. He underwent a routine procedure for his chronic heart issues, and there were complications. He was hospitalized and in critical condition. I told Joseph that I would go with him to California to be with him and his family, but he refused. His family also refused. They knew how important this show was to me and would not let me miss my first one. The show didn't matter to me anymore. Something that had been so big in my life had shown itself to not be the size I thought it was after all. I wanted to be with Joseph, but he insisted that I stay and do the show. I wasn't going to fight with him. He was going through enough, and I didn't want him to bring the guilt of me missing the show along with him to his family in crisis.

Joseph watched me do my first show, and then he boarded a plane to California to be with his family, to sit in waiting rooms and sing

---

* I want to talk about the phenomenon that happens when you tell another woman that your skirt has pockets and they lose their minds, as if instead of saying "pockets" you said, "My skirt goes down on me like a soft boy with something to prove." My personal theory about why this reaction occurs is that women are excited we are finally allowed to have things that we could put in pockets, which means that equality will one day arrive and we can walk around with it neatly tucked on our sides. In reality it's likely we got pockets because fashion decided as of late that big butts and curvy hips are in style, and pockets accentuate that. Sorry, ladies, the only thing that we get to have is just the continued dictation of what our bodies should look like by people in rooms that we will never get to enter.

songs with his very sick dad, who was now awaiting a heart transplant. Backstage before my first show, I was jittery. I wanted and trained to do this show for years. My family, my friends, and my boyfriend who was sacrificing his time with his family were all there, just for me. Just to see if what I had been obsessing over was something I could rise to, and to be there to catch me if it wasn't. My mentor, Jacq, gave me some advice before the show when I told her I was a little nervous. She told me a story about how Judy Garland was known to have debilitating stage fright, and one night before a performance a stage manager walked past her dressing room and saw her in the mirror pointing at herself with a determined wild look on her face saying, "Fuck 'em, Judy, fuck 'em!" over and over again. That advice really helped. I pointed at myself in the dirty backstage theater mirror, I saw my red lipstick, my determined-yet-wild face, I pointed and I said, "Fuck 'em, Judy, fuck 'em!" and I felt invincible. It was a good show. I survived it. That show is something it takes years to get great at. I felt good about my first step up the ladder to that greatness.

Joseph was in California for a week keeping in touch with updates by phone as best as he could. His father's condition had somewhat stabilized, so Joseph returned to New York the following weekend with plans to head back out after the transplant. I left cookies in his fridge so he could come home to something sweet. I barreled into my second weekend of performance, new plays and the same blue socks. We stayed out late after the Saturday show, and we woke up Sunday morning to missed calls and voicemails from Joseph's family. Joseph called them back and they told him his father had died overnight. I stroked his back as he talked to his mom; he just repeated "I'm so sorry" over and over again. There was a lot of crying. It's a reflex when you see someone you love in so much pain to start crying along with them, a reflex I would exercise a great deal in the coming weeks.

The morning we got the call, after an hour of alternating holding him and crying, with discussions of logistics on how and when to get to California. I needed a cigarette, so I stood outside Joseph's apartment on Bedford Avenue and North Fifth Street. Bedford Avenue was quiet on Sunday mornings then, a handful of people calmly waking the street up, hosing down the sidewalk, emptying mop buckets, the blind man who lived above the funeral home next door walking home from church, the *click-clack* of his stick against the sidewalk, the streets quiet enough for him to guide his way home through sound, no French tourists clogging the sidewalks, no movie trucks closing down the street, no strollers clamoring up to the doors of the yet-to-be-built Whole Foods, just a young woman, in a pink nightdress and no bra on her second cigarette of the morning calling her new boss at the Neo-Futurists and telling him, with the stoic voice of a person who must keep it together because they are not the one who gets to fall apart, that she needed to miss rehearsals that week and she would do her best to be back for the show.

We went back to Jersey so I could pack for the week and to be with my family to support us until we could be with his. I packed one carry-on bag, a few dresses and leggings, costume designing myself for a role that I was not sure how to play. I spent the month prior costuming myself for the role of playing myself onstage, and my biggest concern was about my ass crack. Now I was hesitantly costuming myself for my new role as Joseph's rock, and my concerns were far more serious. Did I have what it took to be there for him? Would he ever be the same? Would the way I looked or acted be an embarrassment to him or his family? My role was to be by Joseph's side. A role that I had loved playing for the past two years. This time wasn't as simple as that—he was a different person now, with different angles and needs. He needed me to be someone more for him. I started with the basics: be there for him physically, hold his hand and let him fall asleep with his head on my chest while I rubbed his back. Next was being of service, finding ways to help him through conversations with people he barely knew who wanted to express their condolences. Help with the chores, make food, set up folding chairs, have tissues in purse, hold space. I trusted in myself to learn the part as needed. I was new to his family and trying desperately to not be some random girl in a T.J. Maxx sale rack sundress intruding on their grief, while still being there for Joseph, who I was very much not new to. I was important to him, and because his family are kind and good people, I was important to them.

After the funeral Joseph and I sat alone in the courtyard of his synagogue. He needed a moment away from other people. At this point in our relationship, I was not other people. We looked up at the sky, him in a green button-up shirt and me in my sensible black dress. I remember him saying he could see himself spending the rest of his life with me. I felt the same way, but I changed the subject, not wanting to pull the future of our relationship into this complicated emotional place, as if that was even a possibility. A loss this big becomes a part of your relationship, it takes it somewhere new. I sat beside him, and eventually we went back inside and into the funereal traditions that would make up the rest of our week. I was changed by stepping into this role, our relationship was changed. He saw me as someone who would be there for him no matter what, I saw myself as someone who needed to be there for him. Our fit together was tightening.

The Neo-Futurists sent me scripts and a video from rehearsal so I could learn a new dance piece. We welcomed the distraction of dispatches from an outside world where there were no covered dishes, out-of-place dark-colored clothing in summertime, and crying jags that surprised you from out of nowhere. I would be back in New York in no time dancing on a stage for a laughing audience, a world that felt so far away it didn't seem possible.

The girdle from my audition piece is still in my dresser. I haven't worn it in years. I'm still not ok with my body, but girdle technology has advanced, and I have different torture devices to smush me around now. Maybe one day I'll throw it out, all of it. The blue socks are still in my sock drawer; the bottoms of them are completely gone. I wore those same blue socks for every performance for five years until they fully wore out and another Neo-Futurist convinced me that it wasn't the socks that made us have a good show and that it's ok to let worn-out things go. The leg warmers—the most embarrassing, whereabouts presently unknown. I still perform that tap-shoes play and got to wear them a lot. I've come a long way since badly tapping in Joseph's kitchen. I've badly tapped for audiences all over the US and the UK. As for the pink nightdress and the sensible black dress, I wanted to burn both of them as I unpacked after California, but I just stuck them in the back of my closet. A few years later as I was packing up to move, I put them in the giveaway pile. The clothes went away, but the grief stays. When someone is paging through a rack in a secondhand store they cannot see me wearing that black dress at Joseph's father's funeral, or crying into my cigarettes in my pajamas on a Williamsburg street, a street that woke up just slightly different so many mornings that it is functionally no longer there. They cannot see me doing piles of dishes just to keep my hands busy, just to keep helping, just to feel less useless in the face of something for which I can be no use. They cannot see Joseph and me being there for each other in times of big scary good and times of big scary bad. They see who they will be when they wear it, and I hope for them it's very different from the role for which it costumed me. I hope that it covers their long ass crack just as well.

2012

Joseph

AFTER MY FATHER DIED, it became harder and harder to muster even the appearance of concern for my job at the prepaid debit card company. I went through the motions. But for reasons unrelated to me, the company lost its biggest client, the one that had accounted for a good portion of its income. And so, on the first Monday of January 2012, at the end of the day, they laid me off. I was one month short of three years working there. I felt ecstatic and I felt free and I felt broke and I felt terrified.

In that moment of fear and freedom and grief for my father, I started writing a series of paragraphs about a small town in the desert where every conspiracy theory is true. They were the first little stones that I used to build the career I have today. Of course, I didn't recognize them as such. They were merely weird little vignettes about stuff like mysterious lights floating above an Arby's or ghost cars racing at night on abandoned highways. I had a member of the Neo-Futurist theater company, Cecil, record them with a cheap USB mic I'd owned for years. I edited Cecil's recordings together into a test episode, just to see what twenty-five minutes of audio about this weird little town would sound like. That test episode, exactly as I made it, is still online as *Welcome to Night Vale*'s first episode, clunky sound editing and all. I remember listening to that test episode while walking around and around Williamsburg on an early spring evening, past the laundromat that would soon be evicted to make room for condos that would never be built, and through McCarren Park, where serious runners timed their laps, sweating into the chilly air. As soon as the episode ended,

I would restart it. It sounded complete and outside of myself, something better than I had ever made before. It sounded like the beginning of something, although I couldn't imagine what that something was. I sent the test episode to my friend Jeffrey, another member of the Neo-Futurists, and asked if he wanted to start writing it with me. He said sure and wrote an episode about a PTA meeting interrupted by a portal spewing dinosaurs. And thus, all of our lives would be changed forever.

Of course, I also still needed to eat, and so I got a job signing up people on the street for wind and hydroelectricity. I'd carry a heavy folding table on the subway to some stretch of sidewalk in Brooklyn or lower Manhattan, and then I'd spend five hours asking people to stop and give their personal information to a stranger. I was paid per sign-up, so if no one signed up I would work those five hours for free.

Back in 2011, Meg suggested she should move into my place in Williamsburg. I told her I wasn't ready. It wasn't because of doubts about her. The truth was I had never lived alone. It was important to me to give living alone a go. And so, for a few months, I enjoyed having my own space. Then I told her, sure, let's move in together. Suddenly, she was the one who wasn't ready. Meg has a huge aversion to change. The idea of moving to a new city, to a new state, and out of her parents' house finally, was overwhelming, even if it had been her idea in the first place. So, another year passed of me getting the feel of living alone while Meg waffled, until in 2012 she finally told me she was ready.

We moved her stuff in and rearranged the small apartment to accommodate the two of us. We turned the little nook that I had previously called my "junk room," where I tossed everything I didn't know where else to store, into our shared office, our desks so close together that when we were both working in there our backs touched. There still wasn't room for any furniture in the rest of the apartment besides a bed, so we slept, ate, and worked in bed, only leaving when we wanted to sit at our desks for a little bit in high white IKEA chairs. It was rough those first few months. We fought a lot. Meg broke up with me twice, both times changing her mind an hour or two later. Let it be noted in this book of record that I never broke up with her. Maybe it was because I had been in a huge breakup with a long-term partner, precipitating my move to New York City, but I didn't take the idea of breaking up lightly and certainly didn't want to do it impulsively in the middle of a fight.

But we worked it out, and soon we found a way to grind down the parts of our lives that were chafing against each other. We've now lived together in five different homes, plus countless hotel rooms. It is not frictionless, but we have a system. Life is never frictionless. The best you can hope for is a workable system.

Growing up in California, I came to peace with earthquakes, wildfires, and mudslides. Such is the downside to living in paradise. But I had never been anywhere near the path of a hurricane. When Hurricane Sandy made its turn for New York, I was terrified, and Meg wasn't there. She was performing in Iowa with her theater group, and since all flights were grounded, there was no way for her to come back. So, I bought a lot of groceries and hunkered down at home. "There's a naked, scared man in my apartment," Meg told her friends, which was basically true.

Despite the mayor's warning to leave them alone, it seemed a good idea to take in my window air conditioning unit. It was heavier than I remembered and slipped out of my hand. Fortunately my window overlooked the backyard trash heap rather than a populated street, but still I was leaning out of the window in my underwear, holding an AC unit up by its power cord, in full view of the backyard dining area of the Japanese restaurant next door, their patrons watching me lose my grip and drop the AC onto the concrete below. I went to retrieve it, hauling it back upstairs, and, other than a dent on one side, it still worked fine.

My part of Williamsburg never lost power or internet, but still I found it hard to sleep. At one point I glanced outside and saw what appeared to be an entire tree blow by my window. I saw the transformers in southern Manhattan explode. The nighttime went as bright as daylight, the entire sky turning a sick shade of green. I had no idea what had happened. It looked like the end of the world.

As the hurricane wound down, I went out to the street to assess the damage. The twenty-four-hour bagel place on my block was still open. If they were going to be open in an emergency, it was my duty to purchase an everything bagel with chicken salad. I had been lucky that storm. Others in New York, of course, had not.

Even as life in New York City started to wear on me, and even as the neighborhood, like many New York neighborhoods, transformed into an expensive museum of its bohemian past, I still enjoyed lazy weekends in Williamsburg. The sun glinted off muddy water under the new pedestrian piers (briefly closed after the hurricane tossed sections of it into the water). On an early Sunday afternoon, Meg and I would get brunch at the Two Door Tavern, a place with no ambition or pretense besides good bacon and good pancakes. Then we would wander. Past the two-story-tall squirrel spray painted on the side of an auto body shop by a Belgian artist named ROA. Past boutiques that were empty except for three items of clothing, each item costing half a year of our salary. To BookThugNation, a problematically named but exquisitely curated bookstore the size of a closet. They didn't have room for many books, but I liked every book they had. We would wander south until we got glances from the Hasids whose blocks we were invading, to the west until we hit the condo towers along the waterfront, to the east where the Italian bakeries sold cheap loaves that we would tear into while we walked, and then north, past Polish community clubs that would soon be shuttered and reopened as upscale music venues. The neighborhood, like all New York neighborhoods, was in the process of devouring itself, but it still was ours, for the brief period until it once again wasn't.

Meg was the first person I regularly slept with in the literal meaning of the term, and it is an intimate and difficult thing to learn to do.

When I was small child, I would wake up in the middle of the night and scream, "MOM OR DAD I DON'T CARE WHO!" I never needed anything important. My mother tells me that once I called her to my room at two in the morning to ask her what foods we eat at Thanksgiving.

I slept with the lights on, because I was afraid of the dark. I continued to sleep with the lights on through the end of high school, and this total lack of darkness likely fried my sleep cycle.

I would try to fight sleep if I felt it coming on, and so I had to get my brain to focus on something else long enough for sleep to happen. Until I discovered podcasts in college, the answer for me was books. As a kid, I kept anywhere from three to twenty books on my bed. The pile would slowly grow until most of the bed was taken up by sprawling stacks of books, my curled-up body wedged down at the bottom in the little bit of space that was left. Then my parents would make me clear it off and the process of filling the bed would start again. Some of the books would fall between the bed and the wall and stay there for years.

When people ask my mom at what age I started sleeping through the night, her answer is "he never did."

When I was thirteen years old, I was sleeping on my bedroom floor in a sleeping bag. I don't remember why. Maybe I just wanted to. I was on my back. I always slept on my back. It was the only position I found remotely comfortable. In the middle of the night, I woke up. I always woke up several times every night, but this time was different. I couldn't move. I was completely frozen with my eyes open. It felt like

I was buried alive. I had never been so terrified. I found I could wiggle my fingertips slightly, and I did that until gradually the function of my body returned to me.

The next time I went to sleep, the same thing happened. And the time after that. And every single time I went to sleep for the next decade. I didn't understand what was happening to me. I wasn't merely a bad sleeper, now I actively feared and hated sleeping. I would stay up as late as I could to avoid it. But try as I might, I would fall asleep and wake up to the same strange torture. I never thought to seek medical help. I don't know why.

Then one day, years later, when I was home on break from college, I was browsing around articles online and I came across one about something called "sleep paralysis." As I read it, I felt my skin prickle. The article was describing what happened to me every single night. I finally had a name for my torture. I read with a mixture of horror and hope that if a person is prone to sleep paralysis, then sleeping on their back will cause it to happen almost every time. That night, I began the process of training myself to sleep on my side. Gradually, the paralysis happened less and less. The experience also became less scary because of my ability to name and understand what was happening to me. As of writing this, I have not experienced an episode in months, although it could always happen again, anytime I go to sleep. I still don't like sleeping, although I fear it less.

As an adult I have developed a healthier relationship with sleep. The modifier is important. My sleep is not healthy. I still wake up five or six times a night. I still toss and turn, trying to find a comfortable position, since the one comfortable position I had, blissful on my back, is no longer possible for me. I sleep better when Meg is there. We often say that she provides an example for me. Her going to bed reminds me that it's time to go to bed. When she drifts off, it reminds me that this is the time of night when it would be good to fall asleep. Anytime she is away, my sleep habits fall apart remarkably quickly. Within two days, I'm glancing from the TV to my phone and realizing it's three in the morning.

I am as close to ok as I think I'm going to get. And close to ok is, as any adult knows, pretty damn good.

Meg's ability to sleep is legendary in her family. She falls asleep hard and fast. She has many times dropped her phone on her face after falling asleep mid–Buzzfeed quiz. We joke that she would do well on an Olympic sleep team. She also sleeps long hours. If no outside forces wake her up, she can easily sleep ten or more hours a night. My own body starts to get antsy after a max of eight.

On the other hand, because of the fact that I wake up constantly, I'm good at getting back to sleep. My years of constant waking have at least given me that skill. Sure, I wake up over and over, but each time I'm asleep again within a few minutes, listening to the podcasts that have replaced my creeping pile of books. Meg, meanwhile, who rarely wakes up, has no practice in putting herself back to sleep, and so if she happens to wake up at four in the morning, she will likely be awake from then until the sun has risen too far to justify the futile continued effort of sleep. There is also a strange inverse that happens when one of us is awake and the other isn't. Because I am a light sleeper, I do my best to be as quiet as possible when I'm the one awake, carefully setting doors ajar so that there isn't a click as I leave, or gently setting my book down on my nightstand in a way that won't make any sort of rustle or cause anything to clatter to the floor. I do all of this despite the fact that Meg's ability to sleep means it's all more or less fruitless. She'd be able to sleep through my noise anyway. On the other side of things, when Meg is the one awake, she has no sense of the experience of a light sleeper, and so will slam doors, toss things on her nightstand, throw changes of clothes onto the bed, and otherwise make it impossible for me to sleep. They are all sounds that wouldn't wake her up, and so it doesn't register for her that it would wake anyone up. We all act according to our own experience of the world, which may in fact be the direct opposite of what the person we're interacting with needs.

That first bed in which we slept together in Williamsburg was creaky and tiny, a nervy jangle of springs that complained at the slightest movement. I would toss and turn all night, sending the entire bed shuddering. And Meg slept through it. Because she could sleep through most things.

I wonder, if Meg had possessed a different relationship to sleep, would our own relationship still have worked? Despite all of the ways that we fit together, the fact remains that if each of the many times I shifted and turned during the night had woken her up, would we have been able to maintain that intimacy? I think maybe not. There are so many factors that go into a love story. Factors that are tiny and factors that are monumental, and all of them matter. That two people could make their jagged edges fit together, even with a good amount of give and compromise, seems such an unlikely series of coincidences as to be impossible. And the perennially single may tell you that, in their experience, it *is* impossible. Yet here we are. Along with our approaches to life, and our approaches to each other, and our shared years, we also have this: when I wake up for the fifth time that night, and roll over to fall asleep again, Meg doesn't stir from her sleep. It is on such tiny miracles that a shared life is built.

Meg

WE MOVED IN TOGETHER in the early summer of 2012. Before the end of that year I decided to break up with Joseph twice.

I quit smoking in April of 2012, one day after my twenty-sixth birthday. I had told myself I would quit at twenty-five. So, the day after I stopped being twenty-five, I got into my car and lit up a cigarette on the way to work. As I took my first drag, I remembered that I was supposed to quit that day and then the lit cigarette promptly got stuck in my hair as a breeze came through my car window. *I guess this could be my last one*, I thought as the smell of burning hair filled my nose. It felt like an easy decision given my current smoldering circumstance. Forty minutes later, after I put myself out and the memory of being on fire faded into clouds of nicotine addiction, I wanted another cigarette. I didn't know what to do, so I did what any proper millennial would do and googled "how do you quit smoking?" which led me to an app (of course it fucking did).

That first week was terrible, but then it wasn't. The app and a book recommended on the app worked. A few things became clear to me. The nicotine withdrawals were so bad that I definitely didn't want to have to quit ever again. It was too hard to have to repeat. My identity shifted. Now that I was standing on the other side of being a smoker, I could see how gross it was and how bad it smelled. I have no idea how Joseph managed to date a smoker for all of those years. He must have really liked me. I saw how blind nicotine made me to all of this. It was a staggering feeling to see that I was being brainwashed by poison for the better part of ten years. Also, now that I was a nonsmoker and had shaken loose the last bit of my party girl persona, Joseph and I could take the next step and move in together.

The two of us combined were making about $50,000 a year, almost all of it derived from our soul-sucking jobs and very little of it coming from our artistic pursuits. One of the goals of living together was to share expenses in the hopes of having more time to spend participating in and enjoying the bounty that the New York art scene had to offer *and* we could have a sleepover every night. I was barely financially ready to move out of my parents' house. Every month I would have to dip into my savings to pay for rent, health insurance, and groceries. I took a bet that I would eventually be able to sustainably afford to live in New York City before running aground in my savings. The odds of that bet did not look good, especially after my hours were cut at my day job because my boomer bosses couldn't understand that working remotely is, in fact, a thing, and that no, I did not require connection to a fax machine because it was 20-fucking-12 and email had existed for forty years.

I was very nervous to move into a life I could not afford, but my sister Kate gave me some wise advice. She said, "You're making an investment in yourself, and that's always a good investment." I didn't believe her at the time, but I was in desperate need to live in the city, having exhausted myself and my car's suspension system commuting to Joseph and to theater gigs for four years. I wanted to see what my life could be if I fully dove into New York City, not just as a bridge-and-tunnel outsider but as a full-fledged monthly MetroCard-carrying resident. I hoped I could take on more artistically, because I would be immersed in the scene and not scurrying to and from it. So, I packed up all of my clothes and books from my childhood bedroom and drove them through the tunnel and over the bridge to begin shoehorning them and myself into Joseph's bachelor pad on Bedford Avenue.

I also should mention that we were in love. This was not just a business transaction of cheaper rent for him and less commuting for me. I loved spending weekends with him, drinking coffee in the mornings, wandering around the neighborhood, eating bagels and sitting at the gates of the McCarren Park dog run commenting on all of the dogs at play like we were sports anchors broadcasting a combination dog show/nature documentary to each other.* Living together would be like that all the time, just with less traffic and less NJ Transit, or so I thought. Our love was evolving. Evolving from two young upstarts making out in subway cars and dreaming about making art, into two young adults with full calendars fighting in the back seats of taxis, fighting in bars, and fighting in *our* apartment.

Joseph's apartment was sparsely furnished. The only piece was a full-size mattress and box spring he bought when he moved into the apartment two years earlier. It was the cheapest one in the store and all he could afford at the time. It did not have a bed frame. Being that it was his only piece of furniture, that thing took a lot of heat, some of it sexy but mostly the nonsexy stuff like being a couch, a desk, a dinner table, a bookshelf, sometimes even a stepladder. Eventually, he bought a folding table and chairs at a bodega and an inexplicably heavy TV stand at the Salvation Army to round out the set, which, after we carried it two blocks and up the stairs, revealed itself to be made of some sort of particleboard plutonium. That was what we were working with when I arrived with my trash bags of clothes, mismatched mugs, a collection of plays, and my bed frame from college, which at that point had been moved three times, an unheard-of lifespan for an IKEA Sagstua. (We flattened her in less than six months; may she rest, just as we totteringly rested upon her rickety metal frame.) He had a terrible cheap mattress and I had a terrible cheap bed frame; we were a match.

Our work was cut out for us. I rented a box truck. I made a list; I fucking love making a list. The year prior, our relationship survived

---

* I still think this would be a great idea for a TV show. Get at me if you are one of the many thousand streaming networks hungry for some dog park content.

the purchasing, subsequent hauling through New York City, and the installing of a window air conditioner on the hottest day of the summer, so I thought we were ready for an IKEA trip.

And we really were. We beautifully rose to the occasion as a couple. We stayed firmly on the same team as we sorted through the IKEA gauntlet, starting with The Maze of Staged Rooms Distraction, followed by The Hall of Impulse Buys, next The Forest of Fake Plants, then The Hangar of Confusingly Labeled Boxes, and finally The Weekend Long Line of Cinnamon-Bun-Scented Patience Testing. We returned from the relationship-shredding Scandinavian monolith as a stronger, more bonded, and more meaningfully furnished couple. I knew then that we could do anything.

A few weeks later we tested our luck and returned to the Great Palace of Particle Board and Swedish Horsemeat Balls to pick up just one last piece of furniture. It did not go well. I felt like I was solely in charge of the whole getting-us-furniture operation and he wasn't helping. I was overwhelmed. And then he had the stones to complain that this shopping trip was taking too long. I almost murder/suicide drove us into the East River on the way home as I tumbled into an overpacked-car-on-the-BQE-induced rage hole. But I elected to just rage scream at him instead. Relationships are not a straight line.

We were building a home together with every single turn of that Allen key. I dutifully built every last fucking piece of our furniture haul and dutifully threw away the leftover pieces that mentioned anything having to do with anchoring to a wall, as you do.

We loved the location of our apartment, the rent was as reasonable as any total shithole apartment in Williamsburg was going to be, and it was an ok size for what we needed. But it did have some structural issues. The entire apartment had a grand total of four electrical outlets, which constitutes a millennial nightmare. Thankfully we stocked up on power strips and extension cords in IKEA's Hall of Impulse Buys. I spent the next year and a half tripping over cords and cables that precariously plugged into two desktops, two laptop chargers, two phone chargers, two e-reader chargers, a printer, a DVD player, a Roku, a blow-dryer, an air popcorn popper (one of the only kitchen items Joseph owned prior to meeting me), a TV, an Xbox, a window air conditioner, and a fucking blender. It was a goddamned Nikola Tesla–given miracle that we didn't blow that place up with our unrelenting, almost feral need for AC power.

We enjoyed and struggled with our domestic setup. That summer I was in rehearsals for an NYC Fringe show I was directing, a project that would have been way more difficult if not impossible to jump into had I not moved to the city. I loved going to bed with him every night and having him within earshot for any idea I wanted to bounce off him. I loved living in the city. I hated doing all the dishes and cleaning all his man fur off the bathroom floor. I am by no means a clean freak–type person, but I enjoy some semblance of order, especially because we were living in such close quarters. Joseph is not a clean or tidy person. He thrives on clutter. He fails to see that mess leads to time wasted looking for things or time wasted trying to pry melted candy corn off the shelves of our pantry, likely because it isn't his time, it's mine. I often wonder what else I would have room for in my life if I didn't have to spend so much time cleaning up after him. The candy corn chipping alone was hours and ultimately a failure, it's possibly still there. When I complained about the imbalance in our cleaning workload to Joseph, we would fight. I'd tell him that it's an affront to feminism that we don't share the domestic workload. He'd tell me it's not a feminist thing, it's a me thing, that I'm wasting my time cleaning, that it doesn't need to be done, that the candy corn can stay in place. So, we lived in this impasse, with me cleaning and him telling me I was wasting my time, until we could afford a house cleaner in 2016. His career is years further along than mine, but our drawers are organized and I can always find my keys. Not a great trade-off, but think of all the time I've saved not having to spend twenty minutes searching for a matching pair of socks every day. That must be enough to at least crank out an essay or two.

I knew going into this living situation that Joseph was messy. Before I moved in, he had a whole room in the apartment that he called his *junk room* that was ankle-deep with clutter. He had a one-bedroom apartment and kept one room in that tiny space as a place just to toss shit he didn't want to bother to put away or throw out. This astounded me. We turned the *junk room* into our office, where we worked back-to-back all day long.

There's a level of closeness, an emotional shorthand, a casualness that develops in a relationship in private, which we were still figuring out the limits of in public. We were out with friends after a show one night and Joseph made a joke about something to do with New York and I took offense to it, saying that I had grown up here and it wasn't funny. He told me I didn't grow up here and I had no right to be offended and that I grew up "four hours away." Having driven every inch of the roadway from my hometown to NYC hundreds of times, I can tell you with the exact certainty of a surveyor, it's forty minutes no traffic and seventeen miles. He was trying to discredit my NY cred in front of our friends. He was drunk, and he's prone to hyperbole. It makes sense, he's a fiction writer; but as an avowed creator of non-fiction my hackles came up and we fought in front of our friends and then all the way home and then in bed and then the next morning. We were caught in a frustrating deadlock, both of us trying to hold our ground and defend our personas in front of our friends.

I got up the next morning and took a walk around the block and I decided I was going to break up with him. I felt that lightning streak of embarrassment run through me from being seen by our friends as a couple who disparages each other and fights in public. We were on the same team at IKEA, why weren't we on the same team that night? What would people think of us? What would people think of me? I walked back into the apartment and I told him it was over, then I saw the look on his face and immediately backtracked.

Joseph doesn't always read social cues well and can have trouble seeing when he's hurt someone. It can sometimes feel like he's being careless or rude with social interactions. This is not because he is a shitty person. It's just how he's wired. He is never trying to be hurtful. He just can't always read some of the unspoken nuances of body language that most people can. I was learning that as his partner, I needed to help him understand and navigate these situations. We talked it out. He apologized for making me feel embarrassed in front of our friends, once I explained to him that was the reason I was so angry. I apologized for using our relationship as a weapon, as something I could use to make him feel bad because he made me feel bad.

Throughout our first year living together, we both hit the next level up on where we wanted to be on our artistic paths, no longer interning or breaking our backs for other people's art but breaking our backs for our own damn art. Joseph started his podcast *Welcome to Night Vale* and self-published two anthologies. I was a year into being a Neo-Futurist company member, writing and performing every weekend, working on longer-form pieces, directing an NYC Fringe show, and starting to do small tours.

One such tour was in Iowa right before Superstorm Sandy hit. Because all the flights back into NYC were cancelled, I was stranded in Iowa with a handful of Neo-Futurists, two of whom were *Welcome to Night Vale* actors Kate Jones and Cecil Baldwin. Joseph had to brave the storm alone. I'm not proud of this, but this was one of the times I broke up with him. To avoid being fully stuck in Iowa we decided to drive to Chicago to have a better time being stranded than Iowa could offer us. Don't get me wrong, cornfields with Mitt Romney's face carved into them sure are a sight to behold, but we thought we could do better. The following few days were wildly fun: we went to museums, ate delicious food, went on a weed-themed tour of Chicago led by none other than Symphony Sanders, who I would go on to become close friends with after she joined the touring *Welcome to Night Vale* cast in 2014. But on this trip she was just Cecil's cool friend who had weed.

Every hour or so Joseph would call me, terrified, from our apartment as the storm bore down on the city, exploding transformers and setting whole neighborhoods on fire. He was frightened and alone . . . and whining. He needed me, and I was stoned at an aquarium and growing increasingly tired of leaving whatever fun thing I was doing to sit with him on the phone. We fought a lot. He wanted me to stop whatever I was doing to calm him down. And I wanted to stay in my Chicago bubble, my suspended animation world where I didn't have to deal with our city being ruined, my family in Jersey being in danger, the many thousands of insurance claims that were piling up on my desk at my day job. I wanted to stay in the beforetime. I was trying like hell to not get pulled into the aftermath, the new world that I would touch down into whenever they started landing planes in New York again. I hung up one of the many phone calls and walked back to my fun friends who had noticed that Joseph was calling every hour, and I said to them, "When I get back to New York I'm going to break up with Joseph." Then we ate a hot dog and took a picture in front of the shiny bean or whatever the fuck it's called. I felt that lightning streak of embarrassment again. What would my friends think about the girl who is constantly fighting on the phone with her boyfriend?

Eventually, American Airlines called and let us know they could get us on a flight back to New York. Kate and I flew back together, and I went home to Joseph to break up with him in person. But when it came time to leave, I couldn't do it. This little home that we were building for ourselves felt like something I needed to keep working on. I couldn't break it all apart. I didn't want to haul half of our shoddy bedroom furniture back to Jersey just because I was annoyed by needing to be there for my partner when he was having a bad time and I wasn't. I wanted all of what our future had in store. I realized that just because things aren't going perfectly, it doesn't mean you throw it all away. I agreed with myself that I would never break up with him again. I wanted to keep coming home to him no matter what.

That year, I learned so many things. How to live with someone you love. How to love someone you live with. How to assemble many pieces of furniture. How to make a bet on yourself. How to be a New Yorker. How incredibly cruel it is to break up with someone in an attempt to win an argument or to hurt them back for hurting you. I learned that I shouldn't see my relationship through my friends' eyes because mine were the only ones that mattered. And that lightning streak of embarrassment is just like nicotine, another one of life's poisons that blinds you into believing that what someone else thinks about you matters. It was ok for my relationship and my house to be a little bit messy, to be a work in progress, to throw out the pieces we didn't need. Not much in life is perfect on day one, in year one. In the clear light of day after emotions settled, floors were mopped, egos checked, and nightstands assembled, ours was a relationship that was worth saving, worth working on. We spent a lot of that year taking care of and enjoying each other. And yes, we spent a lot of that year fighting and learning how to fight. Because we were fighting ourselves into a new identity as cohabitants, each of us chipping away at our egos and bad habits a little bit, to fit the pieces of a solidly built life together.

2013

Joseph

OUR FIRST TRIP TO the Hudson River Valley was in 2012, a couple of weeks after I had been laid off from my job. We drove up to Rhinecliff, twenty minutes from where we would eventually live, but our move upstate was years away from us then. We were still kids in our imaginations, and this was like going to sleepaway camp on the river. We stayed in a hotel that was the nicest we could afford. It was directly on the train tracks, and when the train came by the entire building rumbled. We hardly left the hotel, drinking wine in the bathtub and marveling at the expanse of water outside our window. I had just been laid off from my first real job in New York City. A month after this trip I would begin writing those stray paragraphs about a weird desert town. That trip was a moment after one version of ourselves had ended, and the moment before the next version of ourselves began. But we couldn't know that. We never know what version of ourselves is next, nor when that change will come.

Sometimes so little happens in the important moments in our lives. The importance is added later, in retrospect. It is only in memory that we can set our lives into the proper context. This trip was important in many ways. It pointed us toward our eventual home. It set us up for the lives we were about to lead. But on that actual weekend nothing happened except two people in their midtwenties drinking wine in the bath and then driving back home the next morning on the Taconic Parkway, a beautiful road and statistically New York State's most dangerous highway, making our way down from our eventual home to our current one.

When Jeffrey and Cecil and I started the *Welcome to Night Vale* podcast, we did so with the hope that at least one person outside of our family and friends would ever hear it. That first year, from June of 2012 to June of 2013, we followed downloads on a daily basis, checking Jeffrey's hosting and putting the number into a huge Excel sheet. The first month we had 3,000 downloads. Our pie-in-the-sky goal became 100,000 downloads for the first twelve months. We were still working for free and had no path to income, but hitting that download number would be incredibly exciting for downtown NY theater artists used to audiences in the single digits. There were some nice bumps along the way. An NPR chat show mentioned us. The lead singer of the band the Mountain Goats tweeted about us.

"Hey," one of my coworkers at our clean energy table on the street would say to a completely uninterested passerby, "this guy had his podcast tweeted by the Mountain Goats." As might be imagined, this did not elicit much in the way of a response from New York pedestrians. So, I tried, "Hey, have you seen this?" pointing vaguely at my table, and that worked way better. The podcast was exciting, but the tedious sales job paid the bills.

On the first anniversary of the show, in June of 2013, we hosted a party in the East Village. One of our early fans had connections at the music venue and club Webster Hall, and he had gotten us the small bar space upstairs for free. About 150 people came. Meanwhile, we had not only hit our download goal for the year, we had tripled it. My mom flew out for the party. It felt like the absolute height of our careers. Here we were, performing at (a tiny bar space within) Webster Hall. The first concert I had seen in New York, just after moving in October 2008, was Amanda Palmer at Webster Hall. There I had made out with a woman who, before eventually ghosting me, had gone with me on a date to the Neo-Futurists, which had led me to meet my wife and all of the people who would make up my world in that new city. And here I was, back in that same venue, but this time it was my own work being performed on the (small side-room) stage. That night I got a call from my supervisor. I had left my shift early to prepare for the party, and so I was suspended from work for a few days. While being chewed out, I slipped on my apartment stairs and broke my tail-bone. Triumph is rarely ever clear-cut.

Night Vale had taken us further than I ever could have imagined. But that's because my imagination hadn't even considered what would happen next.

The podcaster Andrea Silenzi, in her show about dating *Why Oh Why*, puts forth the theory that every long-term relationship in New York City eventually makes a day trip to the Storm King Art Center. I believe it. Storm King is a sprawling sculpture garden a little over an hour north of the city, 1960s-era abstracts set into rolling hills and ponds. It ticks every box. Culture and nature and, most of all, the kind of empty distances that the city never affords. In New York City, the next thing is only ever a block away. Even in the center of Central Park, you are surrounded by stuff. Storm King is less about the art, and more about seeing the art from a half a mile away, set into pristine emptiness. What we come to visit is the space, not what the space contains.

We took our turn, heading up to Storm King and tramping over its glorious emptiness and slightly less glorious blobs and bloops of art. Afterward we went to a winery, as one does before one realizes that New York State wine peaks at ok, and mostly rests comfortably well below that. We drank mead and cloyingly sweet white wines. In my memory it was autumn, but it could have been any season. Memory becomes unmoored from time. I remember the parking lot of the winery, the wine tour bus full of wasted day-trippers, the gravel beneath our feet, the gorgeous hill of vineyards that the tasting room overlooked, but I don't remember when any of that was, not exactly. We set our memory by our senses, and time isn't one of our senses, try as we might. Our trip to Storm King is not a specific date or time of year, but the smell of cut grass and the heat of the sunshine.

In early July of 2013, the download numbers for *Welcome to Night Vale* started to rise. And rise. And rise. Later, we would call this period the explosion. That July, we had 2.5 million downloads just in that month. That August we had 8.5 million downloads. We hit number one on the iTunes charts and stayed there for three months. It was baffling. We had no idea what was going on. Did some celebrity tweet about us? Had there been a news article we had missed?

The answer, we would later learn, was pure word of mouth on the site Tumblr. At the time, I didn't even know what Tumblr was. But *Night Vale*'s combination of an openly gay relationship, a surreal sense of humor, and a work with no canonical visuals so that fan artists could make characters look however they wanted—these turned out to be potent alchemy for that particular community of fans. We printed *Night Vale* T-shirts and put them up for sale. They sold out in one evening, and now we had hundreds of shirts to package. Jeffrey and his wife came over to our tiny apartment, now piled with envelopes and folded shirts, and we spent an evening packaging and affixing address labels. Still we barely made a dent in the outstanding queue of orders. We were in a realm of popularity that we had not been remotely prepared for.

Due to the new demand, we moved the podcast off Jeffrey's personal web hosting and onto a podcast host designed to handle the larger load. Still, the original hosting instantly crashed, and we realized it was because the podcast logo image was still stored there. Which is to say that there were so many downloads, merely keeping a tiny image file on his hosting service was enough to exceed its bandwidth.

There was a profound disconnect between the new life our project had found online, and the day-to-day life we still lived. Online, fans talked about us as though we were at the same place in the industry as Joss Whedon or JJ Abrams. We were Showrunners, people of immense power in the imaginations of fans. But still, each day I lugged my clumsy folding table out onto the street and spent five hours at a time in the wet New York summer heat selling green energy to scrape together the funds to continue paying my rent. The distance between who this new mass of listeners thought we were and our actual lives was dizzying.

As we explored more of the Hudson River Valley, we came to return again and again to the town of Hudson. When we first arrived, many of the storefronts on Warren Street, the main shopping thoroughfare stretching from the highway to the river, were still boarded up, a dead factory town still waiting for its economic revival. But scattered among the vacant storefronts and the hardware stores that smelled of decades-old mildew were extremely expensive high-end antiques shops. It was explained to us by a shop owner that after September 11, a number of the Manhattan antiques dealers left the city for Hudson, turning it into an antiques epicenter in a rural town previously notable for its closed-up factories. It is a town with one supermarket and fifteen boutique bed-and-breakfasts. We tried a few. They all had charming details and thin walls. On one end of town was a kosher restaurant that advertised itself as the last kosher restaurant until the Canadian border, a claim that could not possibly be true. They served up pile after pile of beautiful falafel, accompanied by pillowy pitas that burned your hands as you pulled them open. That restaurant is gone, one of the great tragedies of my life, and so now it is definitely not the last kosher restaurant until the Canadian border.

We stayed in Hudson on New Year's Eve. It was a last-minute decision and we ate at the one restaurant in town that still had reservations available. I considered that this might be the time to talk about getting married. To, at least, start that discussion. But at the same time, the need to get married seemed less and less pressing to me. We were already committed to each other and talked regularly about growing old together. I struggled to see what marriage would add to that, other than making our financial relationship a little easier from a legal standpoint. As it happened, we ended up fighting that night. I don't remember about what, but it was likely a direct result of the nervous tension I was feeling about the conversation we weren't having, and so it didn't feel like the right time after all. But then, no time felt right. I liked who we were as a couple, and messing with any of the moving parts of our relationship threatened to send them off-kilter. But *Night Vale* was about to overturn our lives anyway, try as I might to keep them still.

That night we watched the ball drop in our room at the bed-and-breakfast and listened to the couple upstairs have sex so loud that every guest in the building heard. The next morning, that couple did not come to breakfast, which was their loss. Breakfast was delicious. On a different trip to Hudson, at a different bed-and-breakfast, we drank too much and became the ones having sex so loud that someone tapped on our door and shushed us. But we came down to breakfast the next morning. No one is keeping us from breakfast.

I got an offer from a major television network to buy *Night Vale* while I was standing at a table at a beer festival a few blocks from my house, trying to sell drunk Brooklynites on paying more for cleaner energy. My stomach floated and nothing I did felt real. The disconnect finally became undeniable. I knew I had to leave my job. I didn't have much in the way of actual income from the podcast, but I had been wanting to be a full-time writer my entire life. I figured I would leave my job and then decide on next steps as they came. I wasn't sure where the money would come from, but I felt that there had to be some money that could be made in all this.

That fall we rented an event space in Brooklyn and put up tickets for our first live show. There were 400 seats. We set up the ticketing site ourselves. The tickets sold out in seconds. We added another show. It sold out in seconds as well. At the show, I ran the sound from a laptop at the back of the crowd. I watched the faces of people as they reacted live to the stories we were telling. Up until then, our audience had been silent numbers ticking upward. Now I watched them cry, and I cried too. We were all people in a room, swept up by something silly I had dreamed up when I was unemployed and in mourning. After the show, crowds packed the sidewalk around the stage door, screaming like we were famous. What is the difference between actually being famous, and a large number of people mistakenly thinking you are famous? I was starting to realize that there may be no difference at all, that fame was always a misunderstanding agreed to by enough people. We signed autographs. I had never signed an autograph. My signature is sloppy and disappointing. Two people told us they had flown from London to Brooklyn just to see the show. I didn't know what to do with that information. I signed their poster, and said thank you, and moved on.

Meg and I went to Hudson for one last trip on New Year's Eve of 2015 (that is to say, December 31, 2014. There does not seem to be consensus among copyeditors or any of my friends that I polled about whether that date should be said as New Year's Eve 2014 or 2015. I say 2015 because it is the eve of 2015). We stayed at a bed-and-breakfast outside of town that had a view of the river and served venison sausage made from deer shot on the property. We didn't know it was our last vacation to the Hudson River Valley, because we didn't know what we were about to decide. We had a bit more money now, thanks to *Night Vale*, and so we bought a taxidermied goat head from an antiques shop in town. The goat's head rode in the back of our car and then came up with us to the room. During the turning of the year, we sat in the bath and talked about the future. We agreed we wanted to have kids at some unspecified point. And then Meg said, "Do I get to be your wife?" and I said, "Yes." That is how Meg proposed to me. Five months later we were married. A year later, after seven years in Brooklyn, we bought a house twenty minutes away from Hudson and moved upstate. It can change that fast, after years of changing that slow. After she proposed, we got out of the bath into the chilly air of the bedroom, steam coming off our shoulders, and we made accidental eye contact with the goat's head, still sitting in a chair in the corner.

Meg

IN FEBRUARY OF 2013 Joseph and I went on vacation to romantic Paris. We had a just ok time. It was cold. My high school and college French was no match for the justifiably impatient French of the Parisian. The streets were covered in huge piles of dog shit. I was a newly minted nonsmoker in the City of Lights, so named because no matter where you are in town someone is always lighting a cigarette. This is a ridiculous complaint. Most people never go to Paris. Lots of people never fall in love. Most people step in dog shit. I get it. I hear myself. But it's important to be honest. I had a remarkably nonspecial time in Paris with the love of my life.

Without a real job and some savings in his pocket, Joseph decided he wanted to backpack around Europe for a month. I couldn't leave my job or my theater company for that long, so I stayed home, worked, ate cans of tuna fish, and watched every episode of *Sex in the City*. I didn't really even like that show that much, but when left to my own devices, I make bad choices, like hating being alone so much that I watch hours of rich problematic white ladies talking about shoes and anal sex just so that there is something else in the room with me besides my own terrible mind.

I met Joseph in Paris for the last week of his month abroad. I spent a fuck ton of money (that I saved from quitting smoking) on a plane ticket and a shaggy Airbnb in the Bastille. I took off work, using my sparing vacation days. After not seeing Joseph for the better part of a month, we were finally reunited in Paris. And it was . . . fine. We fought a lot, he was tired from his month of being a tourist and couldn't really take any more churches and museums. I was disappointed every day that this once-in-a-lifetime trip revealed itself to be just big French New York, and even in Paris I was still me. The stakes were too high. I built up so much in my mind what it should be, that I couldn't see it and enjoy it for what it was. I thought I hated Paris. I didn't. I hated that Paris wasn't what I thought it would be.

Change terrifies me. It took me four years of dating Joseph to move in with him. I was so afraid of leaving college that after I graduated I tried to go back and literally live in my friend's closet until my brilliant mother mercifully talked me out of it. Taking risks terrifies me. I never want to be the first penguin off the glacier into the ocean. I like to wait and make sure that the first penguin doesn't get swallowed by a seal. This is both a smart and a stupid way to live your life. That first penguin gets access to the fish before anyone else, but also, sometimes, is eaten by a hungry seal.

I am a second child, and for a lot of my life, I felt safest following in my older sister's footsteps. This is how I ended up in theater. My older sister, Kate, is a talented singer, so she naturally ended up in choir and in middle school musicals. I am not a singer, but she didn't get eaten by seals in her middle school production of *The Wizard of Oz*, so I thought I would give it a whack, and I loved it. My fear of trying something that no one I knew ever tried before is how I ended up with my career and my life as I know it.

When your life is going ok, is it scary or even silly to want to change it? My needs were being met. I had shelter, a crappy apartment where black ooze leaked from the ceiling. I had food, all of the Trader Joe's canned soup we could afford. I had income, a low-paying customer service position with a terrible commute. Yes, these things were not great, but I was getting by, surviving. There was also this other force, the force that said, "You can be happier! You can be more fulfilled! You can wake up in the morning not dreading your day! It doesn't have to be this way! Try harder! Take a fucking risk; if you fail you will fall ass backward into your middle-class white privilege, don't waste that! Your great-grandma never got to be an opera star because even though she was incredibly talented and passionate she was a widow immigrant with thirteen kids during the Great Depression who had to pretend to be a psychic to feed her family, and you have access to $60-a-month birth control, so take those pills, bitch, and rise to your goddamned potential!" That voice is very long-winded, kind of mean, but ultimately right.

A lot of this force for forward motion and increased fulfillment came from Joseph. We would find ourselves in bed after a long day of working several jobs and I would complain. He wouldn't. He would try to solve the problem. He had a confidence that if we kept working hard and getting better at our craft we would get to where we wanted to be. He believed in his work and he believed in my work. I am a pessimist, and I spent a large part of my life as a fat woman. People whose bodies don't conform to the fuckable "norm" are often overlooked for promotion and opportunity no matter how hard they work, especially in the entertainment industry. I was skeptical and scared. Scared that I wouldn't make it and that I would need to keep working all of these jobs forever.

Then something weird happened in the summer of 2013. Joseph and I were plugging along with our day jobs and our writing and performing when almost overnight, *Welcome to Night Vale*, Joseph's podcast, became a Massive Internet Popular Thing. We are still not sure how it came to be so. All we know is that Joseph, Jeffrey, and Cecil made a thing, a thing that was good and different, and now people we didn't know, knew about it. We had made good and different things for years, but this good and different thing now had a following. Teenagers in San Diego were blogging about it. Dads in Ontario were tweeting about it. Kids in London were making fan art about it. All of them were downloading it, and most of them were buying T-shirts from our Amazon store. We had gone from a few T-shirt orders a month to selling out 1,000 shirts in two days. I lost all the skin on my fingertips taping closed the packaging for all of those shirts over the course of a weekend-long sweat-drenched shipment spree from our tiny apartment. I made Joseph take me out to ramen as my payment and as celebration. It tasted like hard-earned newfound success (and pork).

Joseph told me when he first started making *Night Vale* that he thought it could be "a thing." He was right. It was now definitely "a thing." A life-changing thing. We started planning live shows. Joseph and Jeffrey got a literary agent, and Joseph immediately quit his day job. He's a bold guy, and he believes in himself. I love that about him so much. The world would be a markedly more interesting place if all artists trusted in themselves like Joseph does.

It was a great summer. With Joseph no longer selling green energy on the muggy hot-garbage NYC weekends, we went down the shore to my family's place in Long Beach Island. We went swimming and ate meatballs, as the forces of pressure in our lives changed from just getting by to getting beyond by, getting somewhere new. *Night Vale's* sudden rush of popularity ignited a monumental series of changes in our lives. It was something we had no control over. We had no choice but to keep saying yes to all the new opportunities it offered us.

In September of 2013, two of my friends from the New York Neo-Futurists wanted to start a San Francisco Neo-Futurist company. They offered me a job as a founding ensemble member, to spend a month helping them get the company started. I would have to quit my day job to do it. It was a stipend position ($150 for the month plus flight and accommodation*). I instantly said yes and quit my job. Joseph had just

---

* The rest of the cast were housed together in a somewhat grungy commune in the Lower Haight. I was assigned to stay by myself on the other side of town in a rich donor's guest room. I rarely saw or interacted with the donor's family. I would sneak into the kitchen in the late mornings to make myself coffee and grab a piece of fruit from their bottomless fruit bowl, then I would leave for the day and not come back until after midnight to find my bed made and bathroom cleaned by their housekeeper. I sneakily used the really expensive shampoo I found in the guest bathroom closet. Meanwhile the rest of the cast were dealing with scabies outbreaks and 3 A.M. guitar players trying to read their auras. I do not feel bad about this.

quit his day job and was not eaten by seals. I could do it too. I took a chance that I would be able to find a new job when I got back. I trusted in myself, in a way that I would not have even weeks before.

Taking the leap to become a full-time artist was an easy one. It was a huge life change, but I was not terrified of it, unlike every other life change I had ever experienced before. There were many reasons why. The most strikingly obvious one being that I was privileged enough to do so. With no family to support, the only life I needed to worry about was my own. I was in good health and could take the risk of not having health insurance for a few months as I waited for the Affordable Care Act to be enacted. My partner was financially secure due to a weird fluke of internet popularity and could pick up the rent for a few months while I looked for a new job. And I was given a great opportunity after being taught and mentored by many talented artists over the years to become an expert theater maker. I was now able to go on a mission to the Mission (actually SoMa) to help make a new theater company.

I loved my time in San Francisco. The weather was great, and the mellow vibes of the city were a nice rest from the breakneck pace of New York, the city that never sleeps well. I loved the design of San Francisco. Climbing the huge hills earned you gorgeous glutes and even more gorgeous views of the city and the bay. I loved the streetcars and buses; actually getting to be aboveground and seeing the city as I commuted through it was a new kind of romance for me. I felt like I was in an Ansel Adams photo or the opening credits to *Full House*.

There were of course challenges to being away from home. Joseph and I were long-distance again, except this time it wasn't the Hudson River between us but a whole country. The few phone calls and texts here or there helped bridge the gap, but they also served to make things harder because they reminded me how far away I was from the people I loved most. Joseph and I would talk on the phone when we could. I would excitedly tell him about the good days and hear from him excitedly about the constant updates on the early successes of *Night Vale*. He was supportive over the phone, and we didn't run into the issues we had the year before when I was trapped in the Midwest during the hurricane. He gave me my space and understood when I couldn't pick up the phone whenever he called. I missed him a lot, but I loved the independence of being on my own for the first time in my adult life in this new city.

Choosing to be away from loved ones in pursuit of achieving something greater for yourself is a trade. You are never allowed to forget that you are giving something up to get something else. My family dog that I grew up with died my second week away, my first taste of not being with my family during tough times, something that would become commonplace in the years to come. I talked to my family on the phone and we cried as they described witnessing the painful last minutes of our beloved dog's life. They will walk around with that memory forever, and I will not. I was hit with the wall of all-encompassing guilt that comes from leaving your family to care for your dying dog while you add avocado to everything and midday-drink in biker bars. I was brutally reminded of the trade I made, a trade that felt highly selfish in that moment. It made me miss Joseph and my family.

There wasn't time to get lost in all my missings and guilt, because of that traditional and toxic adage: the show must go on. There was the business of getting this new theater company off the ground. If I was going to be missing out on the lives of my loved ones, I needed to make it worth it. I needed to do what I came to do, and I needed to do it well.

Starting something from nothing is never easy. We were very busy. So busy that the raucous and legendary Folsom Street Fair was happening a few blocks over from our theater one weekend and I never came up for air for long enough to see even one person on the sidewalk get peed on by a leather daddy. There were a good amount of long days turned into late nights at the theater in what was then a "dicey" neighborhood, with a lot of day-rate motels and people suffering from mental illness and drug and alcohol abuse on the streets. I stepped over needles, vomit, and broken glass on the way to work every day. People followed me screaming down the sidewalk when I walked to the corner to get a sandwich. I gave out as many dollar bills as my lightly employed performance-artist self could afford. I started using this new app called Uber to be picked up at the door of the theater and dropped off at the place I was staying across town. As a person who frequently stood in the freezing cold outside a theater in NYC at 3 A.M. trying to will the taxi medallion–adorned gods to send me a cab, I thought Uber was the best thing since the Whole Foods hot bar. As a woman with a late-night gig in a new city, I felt safe and taken care of by Uber (what a fucking summer child I was). Knowing what we know now about Uber, I wasn't safe or taken care of at all and neither was the driver or the city or our economy or the city of San Francisco or our planet, but at the time it gave me a sliver of perceived access to the one privilege I did not possess, safety in my own body. No matter how much access I had to the world and to taking bold steps to forward my career, there's always the looming liability of walking through the world in a woman's body.

All of our hard work worked. We found an audience. We sold out shows and we got the company well on its way to becoming the San Francisco institution that still stands today.

At the end of my time in San Francisco, Joseph flew out to spend the last week with me. He sprung me from my bougie stowaway living situation and we rented a nice Airbnb in the Mission. I made us breakfast every morning from provisions acquired at the Bi-Rite grocery store, drank coffee, and memorized lines. One month prior I had been eating spoonfuls of store-brand peanut butter for breakfast while being bombarded with paperwork for flood insurance claims.

We did two sold-out *Welcome to Night Vale* shows at the Booksmith bookstore on Haight Street. These were our first shows after our popularity skyrocketed. They sold out instantly. The lines to get into the show clogged up Haight Street so badly that onlookers started a rumor we were giving out free weed.

Before the show I walked through the line to help retrieve our guest star's sister, who had become trapped in the horde of podcast/free weed seekers. No one even looked at me, they just let the pushy lady with New York attitude through the line. At the start of the show I introduced Cecil and then read the credits at the end. I was onstage for a total of maybe four minutes. After the shows, I signed autographs and took pictures with fans for hours. They called me "proverb lady." (Because I read a proverb at the end of the credits on the podcast. This is not a nickname that I chose for myself, but it stuck. It reminds me of "lunch lady," and I think there's a lot of power in that.) They told me how much they loved the show and how much it meant to them. Some of them drove in from hundreds of miles away. This was a new experience but a natural-feeling one. I felt comfortable in it. I wanted to do it forever.

In the course of a few months, I found myself in a completely changed life, and it was a good one. I did not spend my days explaining the complicated nuances of flood insurance to frustrated Italian American senior citizens who were high on Sambuca and blood thinners at ten o'clock in the fucking morning. I did not wear a single piece of business casual clothing. I did not eat a single salty can of soup at my desk. My main gig was to bring people together and make them laugh. Change was proving to be a good thing, something I wanted to wrap my arms around for the first time in my life, not run from.

In November of 2013 Joseph and I went on vacation to Italy. My college Italian was no match for the Italian of the boisterous *italiani*. It poured rain. Italian culinary delicacies tormented my diet culture–riddled brain. The streets of Venice were covered in three feet of water. But there were no stakes that this trip had to be the best experience of our lives. There was no pressure to be the most in-love couple in all of Italy. We were changed people now, with more air in our lungs and a clearer vision of what travel, even when it's not perfect, can give you. I learned my lesson from our Paris trip just nine months before. We got to enjoy the trip for what it was, with no capitalist-vacation-day-cost-created expectations. It was fucking paradise. We had the best time of our lives.

2014

Joseph

AND SO WE HIT the road.

The success of *Night Vale* allowed us to start touring the podcast as a live show. Meg quit her job, and then Jeffrey did too. We rented a few theaters on the West Coast, booking everything ourselves. The entire touring party was me, Meg, Cecil, and Jeffrey. We rented a minivan and booked a few Airbnbs. An opener musician, Jason, drove his own car behind us. Our first stop was a two-show night at the Neptune Theatre in Seattle. Afterward we went out to sign autographs, and the line took over an hour to go through. We were giddy and we were lost.

At the show in Portland, we realized that none of us had thought to order dinner. The only place that would deliver to the theater was pizza. The pizza arrived midshow, and the event manager for the venue tried to come out onstage to let our performers know dinner had arrived. I'm really not sure what his thought process was there.

In San Diego, our Airbnb was owned by some recent college graduate bros. The carpet was crunchy, the kitchen was sticky, and the only items in the pantry were a giant tub of protein powder and a bottle of Grand Marnier. There was one towel in the bathroom, and it was stiff as a board. The next morning, before dawn, a neighbor tried to see how loud he could rev his motorcycle for an hour while two cats either fought to the death or had deeply passionate sex. After that, we started staying in midrange hotels, where the breakfast is mediocre but free and every room in every hotel, from Phoenix to Paris, is exactly the same.

We had no idea what we were doing. There was no booking agent and no tour manager and no merch seller. We scrambled and did our best to do all of it ourselves. It was exciting and scary and exhausting, and I'm so glad Meg and I were able to be in that experience together as a couple.

During the early tours, everyone took turns driving and took turns navigating. The driver picks the music or podcast. The navigator gives directions. Everyone else stays out of it. But being a passenger makes Meg nervous, because she likes to be in control. And being a driver makes me nervous, because everything makes me nervous. So gradually Meg took over the driving, from little hatchbacks to fifteen-seater vans. I took over the navigation. These are the roles we felt most comfortable in. Meg with her foot on the gas pedal, and me making sure we're going the right direction.

It is baffling to me to think that when we first started touring, Meg and I had been together only four years. More than moving in together, touring is a true strain on a relationship. It has all the stress and discomfort of travel, plus the hazy work/life boundaries and bickering of working together, plus a complete inability to ever be apart from each other, spending all day in a van, then an hour in a hotel room, then all night backstage, then do it all over again the next day. And those first couple of years saw real fights. Still in our midtwenties and having only just started sharing our home, we were putting our relationship through the ultimate stress test. But we didn't think about that at the time. We saw an exciting leap, and before we could think about where it led or how far the fall, our feet were off the ground.

I had never really seen the country. Now together we were seeing all of it. In Oklahoma City we booked the nicest hotel in town because it cost less than a normal hotel anywhere else. A bit of luxury to ease the strain of tour. In Fargo we looked out at the acres and acres of new houses and shopping centers that fracking had built, and we hesitated to drink the tap water. In Milwaukee, we performed at the Pabst Theater, which has the best backstage in the entire world. It has a free-to-play arcade, a full coffee bar, a fridge with every type of domestic beer, a record player with an extensive collection, a full catering spread, and a TV lounge. It was like hanging out in a cool uncle's basement before the show.

Our first time in New Orleans, our venue was a tiny church. They surprised us on the day of the show with the news that they had no amplification system, so we had to rent it ourselves from the local Guitar Center. Our opening musicians, Danny and Carrie, set everything up for us. The venue had also stopped selling tickets after one hundred even though they had capacity for three times that. We were not sure why they had done that. Also, they had no backstage. We huddled behind a sheet they had hung over a dark corner, our only illumination a tiny reading light hanging by a string. But we had done it. We had pulled off this difficult day, and we laughed quietly with relief. The show started, and a few minutes into it there was a strange sound. An awful smell wafted to us from the audience. Then the sound of someone getting up and running off. One of our audience members had puked something truly potent right in the middle of our tiny audience area. Ah well. We finished the show, as we've finished every single show since.

For the first couple of tours, we went to a bar after every performance. Usually the one in the hotel lobby, or whatever was closest to the hotel lobby. If their kitchen was open, I would order food, something stupid like a pulled pork sandwich. During the first few months of touring, I gained nine pounds. We stopped going out after every show, and I definitely stopped eating after shows. Now Meg and I only drink on Tour Friday, which is whatever day of the tour has a day off the next day. When your job is to be the nighttime entertainment for a crowd of people, it can be easy to slip into the feeling that you too are out for the evening. To drink, to relax, and to party. But it's work. And work is usually better and healthier if you are sober and get enough sleep the night before.

A touring van is just sitting in the same tiny room with the same people for hours on end. A touring van is the changing landscape outside, sometimes aspects of nature so astonishing that the pictures snapped with our phones can't replicate the panoramic majesty, and sometimes a disappointing blur of concrete and box stores and fading billboards so boring it feels intentionally oppressive. A touring van is the constant negotiation of when and where to go to the bathroom. The best place to go to the bathroom is Buc-ee's, a chain of absurdly large truck stops in Texas that advertise the cleanest bathrooms in America. The strangest place to go to the bathroom is a tiny bar in North Dakota with no windows, a small crowd of patrons at ten in the morning, and a video-poker machine in the bathroom, facing the toilet. A touring van is its snacks, picked up at gas stations and lunch stops. At first, these were myriad, most deadly of all being the peanut butter pretzels that single-handedly contributed to a good deal of my weight gain in that first year. But gradually tastes shifted to jerky, which is filling and light and often locally made. Every gas station has a jerky aisle, and I've browsed many of them. A touring van is just sitting in the same tiny room with the same people for hours on end, and yet each hour is a little different.

Through the weeks and the months and the years of touring, Meg and I learned. We learned what we wanted out of a hotel. We learned how to get by in different parts of our country and our world. We learned how to eat relatively healthy while on the road. But most of all we learned each other. In the first, true way, we saw who we were at our worst moments, at the most stressful times, when the plane was delayed or almost missed, when the hotel stank of sewage or still didn't have rooms ready at 5 p.m., when the venue was lacking a backstage mirror, or lights, or a single staff member who was aware a show was happening that night. We learned how to be there for each other, how to act not in opposition or as two individuals but as a team. As a member of a unit who supported the other and took care of what the other could not. That never took out their stress on the other, or at least tried hard not to. When, later, we got married, it didn't seem scary or that big a step. Because we had already toured the world. Anything after that seemed easy.

Somehow, we found a British booking agent, and set off on our first international tour. We hired a friend, Lauren, to tour manage. She started to feel an intense pain on our first stop. Two stops later, in Manchester, Meg had to take her to the hospital. We went on to Birmingham without either of them. It is one of the few shows in *Night Vale*'s history that Meg wasn't at. As it turned out, Lauren would need to be in the hospital for quite a long time. We hired a last-minute replacement as tour manager, and Meg helped out the new hire, the start of Meg's transition into permanent tour manager for *Night Vale*.

In Sweden, we played in a theater that was in the hotel, a hotel that was owned by a member of ABBA. There was an elevator backstage that went up to our hotel floor. We called it the Cher elevator. The backstage snacks consisted only of the largest bowl of potato chips we had ever seen.

We played a church in Berlin with a huge Jesus statue on the pulpit. We were told that, no matter what, we were not allowed to touch Jesus. "NO TOUCHING JESUS," the venue manager sternly told Meg, and then we passed the message among ourselves. "No touching Jesus," we earnestly explained to each other throughout the night. No one touched Jesus.

Our flights between Stockholm, Oslo, and Copenhagen were somehow all canceled. I don't remember the details. I only remember that we had to rent a van at the last minute and drive the six hours from Stockholm to Oslo, do a show, then get up early the next morning to drive seven hours to Copenhagen for the next show. The drive to Copenhagen was miserable, and we arrived to find that the promoter had put us up in a hotel that was both inside the train station and under construction. Everyone was grumpy with one another. Everyone was just grumpy, period. Then Meg and I realized that Tivoli

Gardens, one of the oldest amusement parks in the world, was across the street. And so we went and rode the mine cart ride twice (at the climax of which an animatronic cow turns its head slightly to look at you and then you go down the big drop) and took pictures of the flock of peacocks that wandered the park. As the sun set, we got into the tall swings that were hoisted several stories up a pole, swinging round and round. It was not the kind of ride we usually take, but it was exhilarating and it was beautiful, the lights of Copenhagen swirling below us, and for that minute we were once again on the grand adventure of our lives, and then we went back to the hotel in the train station, and then to the dingy theater, and we got on with the business of performance.

When a person who doesn't tour hears that we are going to a town they know, they send recommendations. "Check out this restaurant! This museum is incredible, you should go there!" But the truth is when we pass through on tour, we are not in that town. It may look like we are. But actually, we are on tour, which is a whole different physical space. What we see of the town is only the local midrange hotel. We see the cheap sofas in the lobby and the plate of room-temperature cookies on the front desk that I get excited by and then disappointed by every time. We see the hotel gym, where those of us interested in working out get a quick one in between our arrival and sound check. And then we see the backstage. The backstage is not the fantasy of backstage that you may have. It is usually dirty and run-down. Sometimes it is nice and well maintained. But either way it is boring. Imagine a room with a few chairs, a few outlets, and, if we are lucky, a mirror. You have now imagined every backstage. Once we did a show with a famous rock star known for his big, hard-partying personality. Backstage at our show he found a room no one was in, turned a folding chair to the wall, and sat silently, looking at the wall, until it was time to go onstage. He did his part with all his usual energy, then returned to his vigil in the chair. The energy and freedom the audience sees on the stage is an illusion.

Or more literally, it is a performance. In every backstage of every show, there is, in reality or in essence, that rock star sitting in his folding chair, staring silently at the wall, waiting for his cue to go on.

Not only were we seeing places we'd never seen, but over the years we were returning to them again and again, getting a sense of familiarity and relationship with neighborhoods in cities all over the world. I know where to get coffee and where to get lunch and where the fun bookstores are in Boystown in Chicago, and in Islington in London, and in Fitzroy in Melbourne. They feel like home neighborhoods in some tiny way, which expands and makes more abstract the idea of home. Especially because touring meant we spent less and less of our time in our actual home, a slightly larger apartment in the same Brooklyn neighborhood that we had rented once my first book advance check came in (it had a dishwasher and didn't have black ooze dripping down the heating pipes). We felt both rootless and always at home. The only constant sense of home Meg and I had was each other.

Occasionally we would sign the walls of the backstages we waited in. Some theaters invite this, their hallways covered in scrawls from touring bands and from community theater productions of *The King and I* from 1995. Our lead actor Cecil would draw a character from our show, the Glow Cloud, and we would all sign around it. The years passed on, and eventually we would find ourselves back in those same theaters, seeing those signatures on the wall and realizing, *Oh that's right, five years ago here I was, doing exactly what I am doing now.*

As of this writing, we've done 375 shows over six years of touring. Our biggest show was in Seattle at the concert hall. We sold 2,320 tickets. The only other show that sold over 2,000 tickets was in London, at the Palladium on the West End. We've done 56 shows with over 1,000 tickets sold, and another 82 shows with over 900 tickets sold. Our smallest shows were at a coffee shop in Greensboro that invited us to perform right when our downloads started to pick up.

Cecil and I flew down, stayed at a motel across the highway from the venue, and did four shows of 90 people each. The musical guest was a guy who owned the comic book store next door. He was, in my memory, pretty good.

When we played the main stage of the Sydney Opera House, our parents flew out to watch. We took a lot of pictures, both in front of the building and from the dressing room. It is not the kind of thing that people like us get to do twice in our lives. We've done some exciting things on tour, but it's not the same as playing the main stage of an international landmark, the kind of place that Carmen Sandiego would have stolen. Our security passes, printed by the venue, identified us as "Welcome to Nightingvale." And then, after all the excitement, we did the show. The same as we had done it on stages from Oklahoma to Ottawa. The moves are the same, but sometimes the scenery astounds.

Now Meg's and my relationship in the car is set in stone. She is the driver. I am the navigator. This is true on tour and it is true when we are on vacation and it is true when we go to the grocery store at home. There may be better measures of a relationship, but here is one, and I stand by it: across three continents and countless countries, Meg has never crashed the car and I've never gotten us lost.

After six years of touring, we move with confidence through the world. The two of us can navigate airports and train stations, customs lines and foreign ATMs, with speed and with practiced ability, and mostly without having to talk about it. We know what each of us is in charge of, because we know what each of us does best. We can tell when I'm getting hungry and so am likely to get grumpy. We can tell when Meg is feeling overwhelmed and so is likely to get grumpy. I'm not saying we are perfect. There are still times when travel is hard. Because there are still times when life is hard. And certainly, there are many, many times when touring is hard. No one who has toured for more than a few years doesn't feel the sharp edges and deep shadows of a tour. But we are not alone out there. That makes all the difference.

A picture taken by our friend and touring musician Mary Epworth in November of 2014 sums up not only our touring life, but much of our life together. In it, Meg and I are waiting at the gate of a crowded flight. Meg is in her big red cowboy boots that were the main shoes she wore for several years. My coat lies tossed in a pile on the ground. I'm reading a book, engrossed in some fictional world, ignoring the crowd around me. Meg is fast asleep, her head on my shoulder. In this way we lived our lives and continue to live them. Life on tour is extraordinary, but it is, above all, life. And, together, we learned to live it.

Meg

HOW TO PROPOSE MARRIAGE:

Step 1A: Want to be married.

This is a good place to start. If you don't want to be married, then by all means, do NOT do it. There's no dress or party or kitchen appliance that is worth entering into a legally binding agreement that you don't want to be in.

If you do want to be married, it's important to examine *why* you want to be married. I always thought that one day I would get married. I grew up in a culture that placed a lot of pressure on women to find a man and get married, a culture that reinforced the toxic idea that a woman's value is derived from a man's desire for her. I see more and more that this culture is diluting, and I hope that it continues to do so. Getting married because you are indoctrinated into a culture that values you on a scale determined by a man's want for you is a terrible reason to get married. Even if you are in a same-sex relationship it's important to consider this, because as I'm sure you know, heteronormative mores have a way of leaching into just about fucking everything.

I knew I wanted to be married for sure in November of 2014. I was in Jersey visiting my family for the night and sleeping in my childhood bedroom alone. I called Joseph before I went to bed to say goodnight, and he didn't pick up. One of the strings holding my shit together popped and I allowed myself down the spiral of "what if?"

What if he was dead? What if he ordered chicken kebab because I wasn't home to cook for him and he got too excited because he loves chicken kebab and he choked on it? And I wasn't there to not actually know how to do the Heimlich but still to be helpful in the panicking department? What if he went out to see a show and fell down the subway stairs onto the tracks and was seriously injured and would need a lifetime of caretaking but the police didn't have anyone to contact and he was hurt and all alone?

As I slipped down this spiral, it wasn't fear I was feeling about him being in danger, it was lack of control. I wanted to be in control of what happened to him, but I knew that there is no way to do that. I wanted to be in control of what would happen after the horrible thing. I wanted to take responsibility for him. I wanted to make the chicken. I wanted to plan his funeral and box up all his books. I wanted to take him to physical therapy and make sure he took his medicines. I wanted to be his person. I wanted that decision to be made. I wanted there to be no question about who was supposed to sign the important papers or to pick him up. I wanted to love him for the rest of his life.

Dark, I know, but if you want to marry someone, this is what you are signing up for. It's easy to be there for someone in good times, but actually wanting to be there in bad times, needing to be there to care for them, is a really good sign you want to be married. He turned out to be fine. He fell asleep early after playing video games and not choking on his chicken kebab and didn't hear me call.

Step 1B: Consider the patriarchal and capitalist implications of the institution of marriage.

Growing up, my sister and I would play a board game called Perfect Wedding. I'm fairly confident that in the history of this game's existence no one has ever purchased it for a boy child. I wonder what games boy children spent their time playing? Probably Perfect Fortune 500 Company or Perfect President or Just Ok at Stuff Guy Who Is Still Really Successful.

How Perfect Wedding works is you take turns rolling a die where each side of the die has a different dollar amount on it ($100–$600), and that is how much you are allowed to spend on a category of item (dress, honeymoon, flowers, venue, etc.). Whoever is able to purchase all the items first has planned the perfect wedding and wins the game. I remember the $100 dress being the most tragic thing that could happen to you. I was seven years old. I had been conditioned from early childhood that an expensive wedding was something I needed, something I should start planning before I even learned multiplication and division.

For the bulk of human history marriage has been the transfer of one man's (father) property to another man (husband). Women had little to no agency over who they would be forced to live with and fuck for the rest of their lives. They were traded for parcels of land, livestock, and straight-up cash. How is this system, even in its neutered *Say Yes to the Dress* era, something that a modern woman with the right to vote and access to credit would want to be a part of?

Step 1C: Resign yourself to the culture you live in and allow your wants to not necessarily come from the most considered feminist place. But ultimately decide that it is ok because you are not going to deconstruct a lifetime of societal pressure masquerading as your own desire with one choice. And yes, you understand that you make the rules in your own life, but goddammit sometimes you can just give yourself a break because existing in this system is already fucking hard enough.

This is definitely something I struggled with. My father doesn't own me and has never acted as if he did. He always taught me to take responsibility for myself, to use power tools, build fires, ride horses, and to not be afraid of anything. He never believed that he had the agency to offer permission to anyone if they were to ask to marry me. That being said, I still have no way to square the circle of participating in this institution. Other than that this is the world I live in and I wanted to be Joseph's irrevocable next of kin for life, and marriage is the most widely accepted way to do that.

I also possessed a great amount of disdain for the institution of marriage because of its exclusionary nature. The right of marriage did not exist for all people and as such it became meaningless, and yet somehow incredibly powerful in terms of legal standing. Getting married, in a time before marriage equality was law, was a shameful privilege. One in which I shamefully abided as I hoped and fought for inclusivity.

Step 2: Want to be married to someone specific.

Wanting to enter into the institution of marriage is one thing. Who you are entering into it with is the more important thing. Marriage is a partnership in the business sense and in the romantic sense. It's not having to go through this terrible world alone. It's having someone at your side to make the terrible things less terrible. It's someone to take out the trash while you shovel the driveway. Someone to call the plumber while you go get the car inspected. Someone to take responsibility for loving you even on your worst day. You need to be damn sure that you are picking the person that you would have the best time doing the worst things with.

I love Joseph Fink. You get that, right? I love his silly walk, his furry chest, his tiny hands and feet. I love the way he thinks about things and how he makes decisions. I love the way he forms an opinion. I love how he thinks about justice and society. I love the art he makes and how he thinks and feels about the art he does not make. I love his T-shirts. I love when he bakes and when he brings me coffee in bed. I love how organized he is with spreadsheets. I love how he plans trips. I love how after we watch a movie, he goes on the internet to read critiques and trivia about it. BUT ALSO: He gives money to charity. He doesn't have a bad temper. He doesn't gamble or drink to excess or do drugs recklessly. He has a good relationship with his family, who are lovely and smart people. We mostly agree on politics and can still have respectful political disagreements. He's good with money. He's kind to animals. He's a good tipper. He showers and brushes his teeth regularly. He has a very nice dick. For me this is a really good partner. It will be different for you. Please consider more things than just good dick, but don't forget to include that if that's something you are into.

Step 3: Decide to ask someone to marry you.

If you are ready and you believe the other person to be ready, decide that you are going to be the one to ask them. Don't wait for them to ask you. Because it is your life, and you should ask for what you fucking want.

Not on the coldest day in hell was Joseph ever going to propose marriage to me. I knew that he wanted a life with me, but he eschews any sense of conventional formality, ceremony, or tradition. He didn't attend his high school or college graduations. He doesn't own a suit and hasn't worn one since his bar mitzvah. He eats cereal out of a mug. There was no down on one knee coming my way from him. I was so fine with that. I preferred that. I like to be in control.

Step 4: Get really drunk and tell your friends about it.

It's a good idea to test this idea out on people just to see how they react and most importantly how you react. Try it out on close friends, on family, or people you don't know well at all. In theater, we rehearse our lines in front of other people before we say them to our intended audience. We don't just do this because we are self-important make-pretenders who love to hear the sounds of our own voices. There's a lot of value in saying important shit out loud at least once or twice into someone's ears before you have to say it for the big time.

Joseph and I were planning on going upstate for New Year's Eve. I was thinking of asking him then. I had not spoken this plan out loud to another soul. The day before we were going to leave was my annual brunch with a group of women who I worked on a show with in 2012. As often happens with this group, brunch turned into drinks, which turned into a drunken sandwich crawl around Brooklyn, which turned into a bar crawl and then into a sleepover.

Joseph was pissed that I was partying so hard and that I would be hungover for our New Year's away. He was actively fighting with me this whole day via text. When we got to our last bar, I thought I would try out telling people I was going to ask Joseph to marry me.

We had picked up two of our gentlemen friends by this point in the night. When I said it out loud, all of the ladies were like, "HELL YEAH! YOU GET IT, GIRL! You get that KitchenAid stand mixer!" and the two dudes were like, "You can't do that, he needs to ask you," and these were feminist "woke" dudes (as if I would voluntarily share oxygen with anyone who wasn't). I then explained that I was my own goddamned person and I don't wait around for anyone to tell me how to live my life, and that they should examine why they think men are the gatekeepers of marriage. And I explained the whole Joseph-hates-formality/eats-cereal-out-of-mug thing, and then they got it.

When I heard myself saying the words out loud, they made sense to me. It felt right. I felt a boon of confidence from my lady friends encouraging me, and the same boon of confidence from my dude friends telling me I was doing the wrong thing. And that is the true test, that no matter what you hear from your friends, you still are just as confident in your choice, if not more so. Because the choices you make about how you live your life only need to be ok with one person, and that person is you. Well, until you ask someone to marry you. Then that person gets a small say.

The next morning, I woke up desperately hungover but ready to drive upstate to bag a husband.

Step 5: Ask someone to marry you.

There are lots of ways to do this. I would recommend doing this in private. It is a huge life choice that you want your partner to make without the coercion of a film crew and an entire baseball stadium full of their loved ones watching (looking at you, Kanye). Marriage is ultimately about you and your partner. For me and my partner, we are most comfortable making huge decisions in private. But hey, to each their ownye.

Joseph and I drove upstate for our New Year's trip. We checked into a very adorable bed-and-breakfast just outside of downtown Hudson. I believe it had the word "manor" in the title to really double down on its old-world stately warmth. Our room had a skeleton key, and we ate venison that was killed on the property that morning. It was that kind of place.

We walked around downtown Hudson that afternoon, and I kept circling the question of how I would ask him over and over again in my head. I was definitely acting a little off all day, but I could just blame the hangover (a perfect plan, after all). When we were browsing a bookstore, I found a book with marriage in the title. I thought that maybe I could ask him that way, because he loves books and I love prop comedy, but ultimately I chickened out. I realized that making a big deal of the ask would just make both of us uncomfortable, so I opted for another route, the steered conversation.

We went back to the likely featured-in-at-least-one-Hallmark-movie-about-a-hot-young-Santa bed-and-breakfast and got into a warm bath. I started steering. "We should buy a house up here and move out of the city." Maybe a bit of a big swerve, but we were still on the road. He agreed; that's a softball when you are tucked into a warm bath miles away from the bodily crunch of a packed rush hour L train. "And we both want to have kids one day, right?" Maybe an overcorrect on the wheel. But again, he was there with me: "Yes, we should have kids." Cool. Cool. Cool. And finally, "Do I get to be your wife?" I steered us over the cliff. "Sure," he said. We landed safe and on a new road. We were both still alive, had the framework of a five-year plan, and our fingers where not even prune-y yet. It felt incredible. I got out of the bathtub, ending my displacement of three-quarters of the water in the tub, leaving Joseph in a shallow pool. It didn't matter now how much water I displaced, he agreed to be with me forever.

Step 6: Buy yourself a fucking ring (maybe).

Do it. Don't do it. There are certainly better ways to spend your money, and there are worse ones. The ubiquity of diamond engagement rings is the result of shrewd capitalist marketing by De Beers Consolidated Mines. What a romantic name? The sourcing of diamonds for these rings has a terrible history of financing warlords and insurgents in regions embroiled in violent conflict. But the marketing and the manipulations of the diamond market worked. In addition to being problematic as all get-out, they are a huge status symbol among women who have been indoctrinated to believe that someone needs to place an expensive diamond chip on your hand to show the world that you are worthy of love and partnership.

Joseph bought himself an expensive painting to commemorate this life event for him. You can take his example and get yourself something else nice that you will hope to have forever and pass down to future generations. Or you can not and save your money. Or you are laughing at me right now saying, "What money? I'm about to spend $700 on a wedding cake that tastes as if a cardboard factory fucked a Pixy Stix factory."

I wanted a ring. The years of playing Perfect Wedding eroded any shot I had at bucking this norm. The day after we got back from Hudson, I took myself to a ring shop in Williamsburg and bought myself a $2,500 black diamond ring, a few rolls of the Perfect Wedding die for sure. I wanted a diamond chip, and I was proud of it. I could afford it after spending most of 2014 on tour. For me it celebrated the fact that I didn't need to silently wait around for something that I wanted. All I needed was to be sure of what I wanted and ask for it.

Step 7: Receive a KitchenAid stand mixer.

In the specific capitalist culture I was raised in, this overpriced kitchen appliance is the brass ring of modern womanhood. You are to keep it on your counter in a prominent place. It is a little reminder of forced domesticity in the history of marriage. A small monument to all the women who came before you, who had no choice about whether they wanted to spend their life confined to a kitchen. Like a cross above your bed or a mezuzah at your front door. Your life is better now because you have a machine to knead your bread. A machine that you can *choose* to use daily or choose to never even plug in.

My KitchenAid stand mixer was a gift from my mom; it arrived three days after we told her we were getting married. A few days later I was walking home over the Williamsburg Bridge after midnight. I saw a Hasidic woman with a double stroller running as fast as she could up the ramp toward the Manhattan side. What was she doing out so late? Why was she running so fast? Exercise? Maybe. Running to something? Maybe. Running away from something? Maybe. She had small children. She looked afraid and wild. She was younger than me. I wanted to help her, but I did nothing. I walked home a free woman. I think about her more than I should. I wonder if she has a KitchenAid stand mixer?

Step 8: Live in a new world as a new person because, even if you didn't think your life was really going to change all that much, it did, and that's a good thing.

Creating change is what making big life choices is all about. People will send you champagne and ask if you've set a date. They will see you as something different. You are something different. You've stood up and said that even with everything you know about divorce rates and the patriarchy, you want to be permanently linked to someone else in the eyes of the law. That you believe in yourself and your partner enough to file paperwork about it.

I can't say if this is good or bad, right or wrong, feminist or oppressive. I can say that it made getting a mortgage a lot easier. And it makes me sleep a lot better knowing that Joseph is taken care of by someone who really wants to be the one to take care of him.

2015

Joseph

WE STARTED 2015 AS engaged Brooklynites. By the end of the year, we were married and living in a house an hour south of Albany. That house has, at the time of this writing, been the longest-lasting home either Meg or I have had since we moved out of our parents' houses.

The living room has the look of a hunter's trophy room. Our first piece of taxidermy was a cheap alligator head from New Orleans, the kind sold in any tourist shop there. The second was a jackalope bought at an antiques market in London. The next year we would buy our wedding goat head in Hudson. Now we have six different pieces of taxidermy in one room. "Is it too much?" Meg will sometimes ask, and I'll shrug. What is too much in this world of weirdness and excess? Most of the art in our house is centered on what our friend Mary Epworth calls "creatures." We have a fondness for creatures, and a lack of squeamishness about the cycle of life that ends with the decorations in our living room.

The kitchen is Meg's masterpiece, the one part of the house we completely remodeled after moving in. We hired what seemed to be the most reputable contractor in our area. They promised it would only take a month and laughed in my face when I asked if they were sure it wouldn't take longer. It took them much, much longer, mostly because they sent exactly one (nice and good at his job) Polish man to do all the work. And they only sent him over maybe three days a week. However, the result, when it eventually was finished, was designed exactly to our needs, which is to say that it is a kitchen more about use than about being a showcase for money spent. We rarely order food out or even buy prepared food from the store, so there is a lot of cooking in our house. In the corner of the kitchen is a little coffee station. The ritual of making—the grinding, the boiling, the setting of a timer—is almost as invigorating for me as the caffeine. I bring coffee in bed to Meg every morning. Later she brings me a smoothie in the chair by the window as I read for a little bit before starting work. It's idyllic because we choose to make it so.

Meg and I got married in our apartment in Brooklyn, under the taxidermied goat head we had bought the day Meg proposed to me. We now call it our wedding goat. The only people in the room were our immediate family, as well as Dylan (our friend and the voice of Carlos on *Welcome to Night Vale*), who officiated the ceremony, and Dylan's husband. It felt right to do something so profound in the place where we actually lived our day-to-day lives. *Yes*, we said, by choosing that venue. *Yes to all of this.* Not some grand show of love. Just this. Just our home. Just our lives. I don't remember a lot about the ceremony. It was sweet, and I was very happy. There was a nice spread of bagels. It's Brooklyn. There's always a nice spread of bagels.

One of my dreams since I was a child was to have a library in my home. My parents took me to our local library once a week, and wandering the shelves gave me a sense of exploring a boundless world. Every one of those books was a door to a different place, and they were all right there, ready for me to open. So when we bought the house, one of the rooms was chosen as the library (it also doubles as a guest room thanks to the pull-out couch). The shelves are nothing fancy, wobbly IKEA pieces that we lugged in from Brooklyn. But they are filled to bursting with books. Books I've read over and over. Books I've read once and then put back on the shelf, likely never to touch again. Books I bought ten years ago and have spent the ensuing decade meaning to read one of these days. Along with the books are the kinds of strange knickknacks a good library requires. A photograph of Meg's father on a horse. A photograph of my mom as a teenager, chugging a beer. A clock celebrating Maoism, where the minute hand is a fighter jet and every second is marked by a peasant waving the little red book. The library of my childhood dreams. To be honest, I mostly do my reading in the living room.

We had two wedding receptions. The first was the day of our wedding in Brooklyn. This was for Meg's family and for our New York friends. We found an event space that would rent to us relatively cheap and catered the party with a giant order from the local kebab place. At the end of the night, we did our best to clean up, given that we were both drunk to a swoon. No one did a great job.

The second party, a few days later, was in California, for my family and for the friends we had in Los Angeles. We did it at the same park where my sister had gotten married a few years earlier, because it's beautiful and also you can rent it for a fraction of what any venue in New York would cost. This was a lower-key reception. The herb-scented California evenings tend to make everything lower key.

Our wedding night was as romantic as we had always hoped. Meg ate a bagel from that morning's spread and fell asleep on the couch. I threw up and fell asleep in our bed. They say you should start your marriage the way you want to live it, and we did.

Meg's office is by the front door and is centered around a shrine to horses, a shelf of horse models she has collected since she was a kid. Next to the shrine is her desk. On the day that I wrote this, I was surprised to find it as cluttered as mine, despite her identity as the neater of the two of us. Next to her desk is the printer we've had for years now, still barely chugging along on the few instances anymore where we need something printed. Above her desk are family photos, a tiny bottle of St-Germain so old that it has gone moldy inside, and a Gilda Radner cutout-doll book.

My office is in the basement. It's painted orange because I like the color orange and Meg doesn't, so it's the one part of the house I was allowed to paint orange. In one corner is my desk, piled high with: recording equipment; a picture of Meg from a truck stop in Horse Cave, Kentucky; a hand towel that I brought to sop up some water and then forgot to put back; guitar strings; a little toy pug that I used to keep on my table when I was selling green energy in the city; a second-place trophy from an erotic fan fiction writing contest in Brooklyn; a penholder made from an actual boar's foot that we bought in Italy (we bought two; the other one is in the kitchen); a CD of guitar finger-picking exercises that I haven't gotten around to trying; a reimbursement check from our health insurance that I e-deposited two months ago; and a flyer for a *Welcome to Night Vale* show from 2013.

In another corner are my musical instruments. My father was a musician, and I grew up playing, and so it's always been a hobby of mine. I have my father's acoustic guitar and his accordion. I have Meg's father's bass and mandolin. I mostly get my instruments from dads, apparently. On my guitar amp is a stack of accordion exercise books, levels 1 through 4. In the eight years I've been at it, I've yet to make it past level 2.

The rest of my office is taken up with all of our furniture from New York City that didn't work in our new house and so we just stuck them here in the basement until we could figure out something better to do with them, which we never will.

What finally tipped us into looking for houses upstate was our landlords in Brooklyn. Only days after we renewed our lease for 2015, they abruptly and without warning started a gut renovation of the rest of the building that lasted months. Both Meg and I worked from home, and we got to listen to them hammering and drilling long before and long after the allowed construction hours in New York City.

Ok, we thought. *Maybe it's time to actually move out of this nightmare of a town.*

The fourth house we looked at was the perfect one. It was near Woodstock and had a panoramic view of the Hudson River. No one had bid on it in months. We made an offer and went out to lunch to celebrate. While at lunch, we were informed that right after we sent our bid, someone had bought the whole thing in cash. I still have no idea what happened there. And so we kept looking, and looking. At houses that were run-down and way too small. And at silly mansions, with multiple kitchens and guest buildings and intricately landscaped gardens that we could never afford. We knew we would eventually find one that was right for us. Or we would lower our expectations enough that a house would clear that bar.

On Halloweens, we load up our front porch with decorations. I always loved the houses that went too big on Halloween, that spent too much and cluttered their yards. I couldn't wait until I could do the same. We are building our collection slowly, a few pieces every October. Each year we buy two of the biggest pumpkins we can find and prop a waving skeleton against one of them. We cover the rocking chairs on the porch with cobwebs and put up giant light-up spiderwebs with giant light-up spiders.

In the spring, we hang flowers off our porch, and once a robin, in a choice she would soon regret, set up her nest just outside our sliding glass door in the hanging flowerpot. She would chirp frantically every time we went out on the porch. "Well, we're sorry, but we were here first," we would try to explain, but she never seemed to get it. From the second floor, we could lean over and see the three little blue eggs, in their nest, in their pot, on our porch. The eggs never hatched.

The backyard slopes down to our neighbor's property behind us, which makes it a perfect sled hill in the winter. Being from Southern California, sledding had never been part of my life, so it is an odd thing to be able to walk out of my office and be standing at the top of a thrill ride. The slope steepens toward the end, providing a nice burst of speed that sends you spinning out into the flat field below. Of course, every ride is paired with the tedious trudge back up, but life is, after all, about balance. Or at least that's what we tell ourselves when things get bad.

The moment I saw the house we bought, I knew we would buy it. It had a great view and was nice without being a ridiculous mansion. Meg was less sure, but she came around. We put in our offer, got qualified for a mortgage, and promptly went on a *Night Vale* tour. Before we went, we signed power of attorney over to Meg's father. So, while I have bought a house, I have no idea what buying a house is actually like. Jack did all of that for us. It was during the book tour for Jeffrey's and my first novel (which also came out that fall, a year so full of milestones that I couldn't find room for all of them in this essay) that we heard that we now owned a house. It felt about as real as being told that, somewhere in the world, there was a dragon that belonged to us. A nice story, but we'd believe it when we saw it.

What finally convinced Meg that this was the right house was the master bedroom. It is bigger than any apartment we had in New York City, and it's on a different floor from the rest of the house, which adds a feeling of further isolation to the isolation of the woods. From our bed we can see the Catskills out across the valley, and at night the red blinking lights at the tops of the hills. We never bothered to put curtains up, so the room floods with morning light. The two of us took to sleeping with masks. With the lack of curtains, I'm sure the neighbors have seen us naked more than once. Good for them.

The only issue is the stairs up to the bedroom. Meg isn't great on stairs, and we always are afraid that she will die falling down a staircase and then I will go to jail because no one will believe it was an accident. In fact, the opposite almost happened. Soon after we moved in, we were dancing near the staircase, and I leapt into her arms. She dropped me, and I fell headfirst on the bottom step. I was ok, but we realized that it was the first day that my new life insurance had kicked in. If by some horrible turn of fate I had died in that fall, Meg would definitely have gone to prison.

On the day we moved in, we arrived to find the cable installer and the mattress delivery truck in our driveway, and Meg realized she had lost the only copy of the house key. So, she found a window we had left unlocked and crawled through the window to let us all in. We researched and found that we were in the delivery radius for exactly one restaurant, a pizza place, and so for the first and last time in this house we got a pizza delivered. We ate it on the floor, surrounded by boxes full of everything we owned, and wondered what the hell we had gotten ourselves into.

"Take me home," Meg said to me, meaning Brooklyn, meaning a simpler time in our lives when we weren't responsible for a house, meaning she was afraid.

"You *are* home," I said, meaning this house, meaning this town, meaning us, meaning our lives together, meaning I was afraid too, but we could be afraid together.

Meg

THERE ARE SEVERAL THINGS you should know about driving a 12 ft. tall 23 ft. long Sprinter van all day every day for two months:

1. It's very big.
2. It's sometimes a metaphor for growing up.
3. It's sometimes not a metaphor, but a literal two-ton chunk of metal that is your sole responsibility.
4. There is no bathroom in the van, but you can start a rumor mid-tour that there is one. It will lead to much confusion.
5. It is almost completely impossible to park anywhere.

In the late winter of 2015, with my hard-earned engagement ring on my hand, I set forth to plan the most challenging event of my life—the 2015 *Welcome to Night Vale* forty-three-city-long US spring tour.

After touring with *Night Vale* in 2014, I realized that I loved touring, that I loved performing my jokes, wearing my costumes, and playing the character Deb, a sentient patch of haze, but that I wasn't being challenged enough and I wanted to take on more responsibility on the road. I asked to be considered for the tour manger position and they fucking hired me. I had some experience. I had been on a tour before and I stage-managed a production in college and two very robust children's musical theater shows in high school, but I didn't know shit about shit. And, even worse, I didn't know that I didn't know shit about shit. I needed to learn fast.

This was before I knew about many things, like about how the oatmeal at the Hampton Inn breakfast varies in consistency depending on what time in the morning you go to the buffet. Let me break it down for you: 6 A.M. water, 7 A.M. watery mush, 8 A.M. perfect, 9 A.M. glue, 10 A.M. gone. It was before I knew how to do an eleven-point turn without screaming in frustration after wheel-cut seven. I didn't know that promoters are always trying to lightly steal from artists and it's the tour manager's job to steal back. I did know it was my job to get our show to forty-three cities and back in a very large vehicle, a vehicle that I was afraid to drive. I also knew it was important in a leadership position that I show no fear.

The van came with a name, Hilda. It also came with a speed governor, so no matter how hard you pressed that gas pedal you were not going above 82 mph—which is a nice safety feature unless, you know, you needed to change lanes or pass someone. Something you would never need to do on a 15,000-mile road trip. It felt like I was in a bad first draft of the movie *Speed*.

Two cities into the tour, a roadie for another show dropped a large piece of movable metal fencing on Hilda. They say, and by *they* I mean Sheryl Crow, the first cut is the deepest. From then on, every other scratch became less of an issue. You don't want to be the one to take the first slice out of the cake, y'know, so luckily some roadie in DC got us rolling with ripping up that van. I was averaging a scratch a week. Curbs, gates, walls, cars, and poles were all in danger. I hit everything but the lottery with that van. About two weeks into the tour, I clipped the promoter's car while they were watching as I was pulling up to the venue. I got out and said nothing, they said nothing, and we went on with our night. I am always great at first impressions.

I'd like to be able to tell you that at this point in the tour I was finding my footing and enjoying the challenge of being tour manager, but that is a great untruth. My shitty driving was the least of my problems. It's hard being new at something. It's hard when you are new at something and you feel like you are working without a net. I have trouble letting people help. I would rather push myself to the edge and do all the work to be the one in charge than share some of the responsibility and risk someone fumbling. It makes me very tired, very frustrated, and very lonely.

I remember standing outside of a Hampton Inn in southern Florida and realizing that by the time we got to Portland, Oregon, in three weeks *that* would be the halfway point. I remember screaming at the sky, "How is this not over yet?!?" I'm not sure if I meant the tour or my life.

When we pulled into Los Angeles my nerves were shot. I hadn't slept more than a few hours a night for a month straight. I was still trying desperately to show no fear, and my hands had started to shake uncontrollably. When we got to the hotel in Hollywood, the van did not fit in the parking structure because of course it fucking didn't. I dropped everyone else off at the hotel to rest. Then I drove around in Friday afternoon downtown LA traffic for an hour trying to find a lot that would take the beast. I finally found one that said they could keep Hilda for a few days and we could come and go as needed. I got back to the hotel. I had ten minutes before I had to drive to load in. Then I got a phone call from the parking lot. They forgot they had an event the next day, I needed to move the van, and I couldn't park there overnight. I cried. Also it was my birthday. I was twenty-nine.

Everyone has a tour bottom. LA was mine. But the show must go on, and it did. Joseph found me in a puddle in my dressing room, crying and shaking and buried under the giant pile of scripts I was printing for all our Los Angeles guest stars. He looked me in the eyes, told me "the only way out is through," and then he began helping me collate. I got dressed and performed my jokes to a sold-out audience at the Orpheum, phoning in what was the opportunity of a lifetime because I was too worried about where to park a fucking van to give all of my attention to the art. I definitely was being challenged enough now.

We had the next day off, but there is no real "off" when you are a tour manager with an act on the road. There are always emails to send, a bank run to make, a lost FedEx package to retrieve from a faraway airfield, or an oil change on a two-ton albatross needed. But for this day Joseph stepped in and pulled the "It's my company and you need to actually take the day off or your eyes will never stop looking like you're trying to unsuccessfully shit a Sprinter van," and I listened. Joseph delegated the van situation to our merch manager, took me out of our shitty tour hotel, put me in a Lyft, and whisked me away to a surprise location.

We pulled up to the Hotel Bel-Air. It smelled like lavender, and the air felt soft and warm. The hotel greeter who creepily knows who you are as you walk up called me Mrs. Fink and I didn't even bother to correct them. We had a full day couples' spa treatment including a lunch of spa food, which is just vegetables steamed in affluence. I saw David Schwimmer at the hotel pool; he wasn't schwimming (I'm so sorry), he was chatting up some very babeish lady bikini babes, who were coated in that LA-model disinterested cool like they never had been excited about a thing. It was a truly magical place, which I didn't know at the time is problematically owned by the Sultan of Brunei, who backs laws that torture LGBTQ people, so don't ever go there ok and I won't ever go back because that's a real turd in the Wolfgang Puck–crafted punch bowl.

Joseph booked us an incredible room with its own pool, so I wouldn't have to share with Ross and the bikini babes, because that would send me into a body shame spiral so powerful it would turn the Olympic-size swimming pool into a whirlpool of self-hatred. Joseph gets me. He sees how hard it is for me to be in bathing suit situations and always goes out of his way to make me feel normal. He's reassuring without being patronizing. He doesn't say, "You're the most beautiful perfect woman," because he knows that's not what I need to hear. He says just a simple "You're ok, Bear, you're ok, it's gonna be ok" when he sees me start to lose it in front of a mirror. That helps.

After we settled in our room and did all of the hotel sex things that you do, we were in our robes, I looked at Joseph and the sun was coming through the window, and I felt with every pound of my flesh that I loved him. I knew that I had loved him before; I asked him to marry me, for fuck's sake, but this was new. I was in such a terrible place of stress, risk, exhaustion, and inadequacy, and he helped me. I was on fire, and he took me to the spa where they put me out with face masks, lavender massage oil, and $70 omelets that were only ok. He took care of me, just as I wanted to take care of him forever. I never really thought about that aspect of the eternal love and partnership. I knew I wanted to be there for him; it is just this huge added bonus that he wants to show up for me and treat me to lavish accommodation and general flouncyness.

It was a ridiculous extravagance. One that I never would have spent for, myself, but I was pouring everything of myself into this tour and what was pouring back was money, enough money to go fuck off for a day and not have to deal with any harsh surfaces or issues. I did have to go back to the tour, though. I'd like to say I was renewed and refreshed and ready to take on another month; I wasn't, but I was tremendously grateful for the day I spent on the outside. I got back in the van. The only way out is through.

Eventually we got to Portland, my halfway beacon of hope, and it started to get easier. I started delegating small things. The shaking in my hands eased up. I made deals with parking lot attendants. I felt no guilt when scraping the van against concrete poles. I parallel parked in busy downtowns and did not give even one small fuck about the traffic behind me. They can wait. Honk all you want, sir, because YOU ARE GOING NOWHERE. I was getting a handle on the job. The days were still full to the point of explosion, but I began to calibrate to the pressure.

My friend and fellow *Night Vale* cast member Symphony and I went to my favorite dress shop and bought some new outfits for shows on a morning off in Portland. At this point we were sick of everything in our suitcases. I found a dress I thought might be good for my wedding. I pulled it off the rack and it fit great. I texted my mom and sister a picture, and my mom texted back, "I'm crying, I wish I was there with you," and I was like, "shit, is this supposed to be a big deal?" It wasn't. It cost a hundred-fifty bucks and I got a red veil for ten dollars. I threw it in my suitcase and then went out for morning drinks with Symphony and Joseph.

Yes, during this massive career-growth process, I was planning a wedding. The wedding was the easiest part. A tour manager puts on a wedding a night, between the venue rental, the ticketing, the budgeting, staff coordination, staging, and the coordinating catering; it's all the same bag o' chips. An actor can put themselves into makeup, hair, and costume in less than an hour, get up and talk in front of thousands of people, and confidently be the center of attention—that's what being a bride is. I had this in the bag, so much so that we had two weddings, one in Brooklyn and one in Los Angeles. A life in the theater prepares you for so much more than wearing tights and talking loudly.

Mercifully, the tour ended. The last day on the road included a touch-and-go moment of being on a road with a height restriction that our van was too tall for, but we figured it out. We had to. The tour doesn't end until you get to the end. We pulled back into Brooklyn. The only parking spot available was next to a fire hydrant in front of my apartment. I sat and waited three hours in the cargo hold of the van for the rental company to pick her up so I wouldn't get a ticket. I was mere feet from my home but still trapped in that fucking van, sitting shiva for the tour that tried to kill me. Eventually they came and took her away. I was not sad. A 12 ft. tall 23 ft. long weight had been lifted off of my shoulders.

I took a shower. I cooked food. I slept in my bed. I didn't think about heights of parking garages or boxes of T-shirts or what it means to show fear. I drove my Volkswagen Golf around and wedged it into tiny spaces with the greatest of ease. But something had switched in me; I started planning our next tour. I couldn't wait to get back on the road and keep getting better at the job. I had been through tour boot camp, and now I was hungry for more combat with vans, mean sound dudes, and questionably textured hotel oatmeal. I'm a masochist and a bossy-ass bitch, you saw this coming.

Three weeks after returning from tour we got married. I was so busy putting everything together that I sorta phoned in my vows, just like that night at the Orpheum. I regret that. Joseph's vows were good, but then again, he didn't have to spend time fighting with anyone on the phone about tablecloths, so there's that. He vowed that no matter where we were in the world, we would always be home if we were together. I agreed. If I had to do my vows all over again and I can't but I do have this book so I'm going to shoot my shot: Joseph—I promise to always consider you.

That's much cleaner than the rambling mess I put forth while I was actually thinking about whether there would be enough chairs at the reception. I know it sounds simple and maybe not enough, but to me it is tantamount to any other flowery declaration of love I could bloom forth. Always considering him, his feelings, his happiness, his well-being in every aspect of my life is what I endeavor to do as his wife.* It's all encompassing, from remembering to buy the beef jerky that he likes to where and how we live our one unique life.

Our wedding day was not magical. It was long and a lot of work. By the end of it I was grumpily hauling trash to the curb in my wedding dress and already hungover. Joseph and I went back to our apartment. I ate two bagels and fell asleep on the couch. Joseph threw up and then slept in our bed. Very romantic. The next day I went to the grocery store and bought ingredients to make a nice dinner for the two of us. Making dinner for my husband was magical. Knowing that I would get to do that for the rest of our lives was magical. Starting day one of our new plan for our forever was magical. If our plan works, I will make him dinner thousands of times. This felt more meaningful

---

* He referred to me as his partner once, and I sternly replied, "This isn't a law firm, I'm your fuck hole."

to me than a white dress and a champagne toast. This was an action, an action of love and care. The commitment to everyday acts of love and consideration is the reason we did all this wedding bullshit.

We went to California the next week for our LA reception, which was way more mellow. I didn't do as many shots, and I didn't have to haul hardly any trash. Then we were off to Hawaii for two fucking weeks for our honeymoon. Having a DIY wedding on the cheap allowed us to really splash out on the honeymoon. I fully recommend this tactic.

We met this hippie couple in the fancy-person lounge at our hotel, and they gave us a brick of hash and a big-ass jar of weed. The two of us didn't really smoke anymore, but we decided to give it a whack. I rolled us a joint using pages from the King James Bible lovingly placed by the Gideons for salvation and spliffs. We took a few hits, got way too stoned, and went for a walk on the beach at sunset. The warm water felt incredible on my legs. The sun melted into the sparkling sea. I held my husband's beautiful hand and had the sudden sinking feeling that if all goes to plan with our lives, I will watch him die. I thought about what that might feel like. Then I thought about ordering a barbecue chicken pizza when we got back to the room.

That is what being married is all about for me—having someone to be with you when you are dying and also having someone there to say, "Can we get curly fries too?" when you order your room-service pizza.

There are several things you should know about getting married:

1. It's a very big deal, whether you want it to be or not.
2. Weddings are a special day, but I've had many better days in my life, many of them in Hawaii, where neither of us threw up.
3. The honeymoon is the most important part.
4. Don't phone in your vows because you are distracted by details.
5. Being married doesn't make you a grown-up. Being a tour manager does.

2016

Joseph

WE WERE IN LONDON because Meg was helping a friend start a theater company, and we were in London because it seemed like an adventure and we had decided we were people who liked adventures, and we were in London because nowhere and everywhere felt like home, and so why not have that home be abroad for a little bit? For these reasons, and probably for other ones, Meg and I spent the fall of 2016 living in London. It turned out to be a miserable time.

The flat we rented was a little tangle of a place. A narrow hall to a bedroom, then another narrow hall to a small kitchen and living room. The closet was locked, and the owner had left us a flimsy portable wardrobe to store our clothes. The apartment had a deeply confusing address, involving half numbers and a letter at the end. On the first night there we tried to order Indian delivery. The delivery guy just could not find our apartment. I stood outside, on the phone with him, as he moved around and around our neighborhood, never listening to the directions I gave. After an hour of this, I called the restaurant to try to coordinate. The person at the restaurant said, "What do you want me to do? Am I God?"

Certain cities in the world are twins of each other. Dublin and Boston, for instance, are the same city (strong literary scene, lots of Irish people, deeply bleak and boring). Seattle and Stockholm also (cold and gray climate, warm and welcoming architecture, good coffee). London and New York are so much the same city that some of their neighborhoods have the same name. They are so much the same city that I'm pretty sure you could use a map of New York to navigate

London. In this way I both felt immediately at home in London, after my years of living in New York, but I also didn't find it as exciting as international living might sound, since it felt like a city I had already left behind.

Gradually we settled into our neighborhood. For exercise we would go running along the nearby canal. The canal is home to hundreds of houseboats. Some are elaborate crafts with roof decks and clean modern lines. Others have the look of tugboats from old picture books. One smelled of burning plastic all the time. The canal was this little floating city, snaking its way through the gray high-rises of London. This was the kind of idea that would never be allowed if it were proposed in the modern day, only allowed because it has always been this way and who's going to change it now?

Running, Meg and I learned, is a great way to interact with the world as you travel through it. You get to know a city outside of work or tourism. All that matters is the distance and the loop, and so your path takes you through unlikely places you would not have otherwise seen.

There were fine points of etiquette it was easy to get wrong in London. For instance, in America, the emphasis of politeness in customer service situations is in the "thank you." "Could I get a glass of water? Thank you." We regularly even say thank you before the service has been rendered. The request is casual, but the gratefulness we express is codified. In the UK, it is the exact reverse situation. The "thank you" is optional, but to leave out a "please" is deeply rude. Any food or drink order that did not include a please would be responded to with a long glare, as though the bartender was the mother of a four-year-old, teaching them "what do you say?" before handing them more mac'n'cheese. That we said "thank you" after did not mollify them. In fact, it hardly even registered. How much of perceived rudeness of others is merely a misunderstanding of their cultural terms?

We were in London while I was on final deadline for a book. I spent a lot of that time in a haze of stress that was only exacerbated by how difficult it was to get any normal human errand done in a country we didn't quite understand. Grocery shopping became a hunt for a single green vegetable in the sparsely stocked London markets. Navigating the roads was a constant reminder to look the correct way or risk tossing ourselves under the wheels of a passing vehicle. And through all of that I also had hundreds of pages of a book to go through, deciding between three different versions of a sentence, weighing the merits of this word versus that word, and looking up both words only to discover that one of them doesn't mean what I had always thought it had meant.

A city is inseparable from a person's emotional experience of the city. We map our lives upon the places we go. In Munich, we were relaxed and happy, so Munich is a relaxed and happy city. In Helsinki, we were exhausted, and so Helsinki is an exhausted city. And in London, I was drowning in stress, and so London to me is a city of stress.

My writing life has been a series of tides. When the tide comes in, and the deadlines loom, I drown, and it hardly seems possible that the water will ever recede and that I will ever be able to breathe easy again. Then the tide is out again, and all of my deadlines are distant, and I once again say yes to way too many projects at once. Meg has her own tides, but they don't work on the same schedule as mine. The goal is that we can each support the other when the cold waters of overwhelming work come rushing in. This goal is imperfect, and imperfectly executed, but we do our best.

Of course, I'm just dancing around the rotten core of this rotten year.

In September, Garrison Keillor wrote a column making fun of the fact that Trump's campaign was doomed. Nothing about that essay has aged well—one outdated sex pest poking gentle fun at another and getting paid well to do it. In retrospect, this was one of the harbingers of what was to come. Because it wasn't just the bad old men, but all the old men. The handsy men in power, who hid their toxicity behind a genteel chuckling mask, a thin veneer of respectability that allowed Keillor to keep his job being not very funny on the radio for years and years, despite what everyone knew, what everyone always knows, but no one said out loud, not in any unified way, until November 2016. The statement of November 2016 was not new information. America just finally said the quiet part loud.

Leonard Cohen died the day before the election. Lucky him. Of all the artistic Jews kicking around the last hundred years, Leonard always meant the most to me. Maybe it's that he was so good at so many things. You have to respect that kind of talent. Or maybe it was because he found the best balance between the myth and the reality. He neither cast himself as a perfect person, nor was he showy about his faults. He simply did his best with life, like any of us, and expressed that in a few perfectly chosen words.

A lot of famous people died in 2016. A lot of famous people die every year. I don't think that year was any different, other than that it became a meme to talk about the year that murdered all the celebrities. And for the most part, I have a hard time feeling much when a famous person dies of old age. I know and love enough finite humans that I don't need to invent more tragedy in my life, and dying of old age is the happiest ending any of us can expect. But I felt Leonard's death.

At least he never had to see what the world would become without him.

On election night, I was as confident as anyone, and that made the blow much worse than it would have been if we had gone in scared. But in retrospect it was just a confirmation of the Jewish view of history. The Jews have been a marginalized and prosecuted people for literally thousands of years, and so we have learned to take any safety and acceptance as conditional and temporary. There is no getting past the outside world's suspicion, there are only brief moments when the hateful eye turns elsewhere before it inevitably darts back to us. Trump's presidency would directly lead to a huge upswing in hate crimes against Jewish people. I didn't know that yet, on that night in London, as we stayed up late to hear the returns, but the Jew in me certainly felt the great dull bell of history, tolling for our blood once again.

That week we went to a bookstore near the apartment. They were featuring a memoir by a woman named Teffi, a Russian writer who wrote about her exodus following the Soviet revolution. I bought it, partly to learn about the past, and partly to get a sense of a possible future. The Jewish foothold in any country is always provisional. Maybe a hundred years was all the United States would give my family. Maybe it was time to learn about what running away forever might be like. And if I had to go, Meg would be pulled alongside me into that ancient cycle of exile.

We had appointments to get tattoos the day after the election, and when the horrible thing happened, we debated on whether to keep the appointment. Would we think about that night every time we looked at the image on our skin? This was before we understood what the coming years would be like. That we would think about that election every single day whether we had tattoos or not.

As it happens, I don't particularly associate either tattoo with the events around their creation. Mine is a quote from *Night Vale*. It says "All tattoos are temporary" in the center of a wreath of flowers. That statement is, technically, true. Meg's tattoo is of a diving horse, like the ones that used to perform on the steel pier in Atlantic City. We later named her horse "Spirit, the Power Horse." There is also a theme song for the horse, most of the lyrics of which are just his name.

A week after the election, we went out for a nice dinner. That night I woke up at 2 A.M. and evacuated everything in my body. I spent the night this way, dry heaving once I was empty, sitting on the couch with a plastic bag in case I couldn't make it to the bathroom. I assumed I had food poisoning. But my digestion would never be the same again. I would have these brutal episodes twice more in the coming two years, and even now am nauseous more days than not. Maybe the stress of 2016 followed by the devastation of the election finally tripped some switch in me, but my body was manifesting the turmoil inside in unfortunately tactile ways. Gradually, the stock of anti-nausea drugs in my backpack grew, until I started to carry a pharmacy on my back every time I traveled. Everything I do now is a negotiation with my stomach, and this started one week after the election, during this awful month we spent in London.

Finally, the month ended. We came home to an America laid bare in its viciousness, in how little it cared for us and those we loved.

We arrived a few days before Thanksgiving. We had agreed to host our family upstate. While we were gone, mice had overtaken the house. There was mouse shit in every room. Acorns hidden in every bed. Every surface in the house had to be scrubbed, and we had three days to do it.

That day, we went shopping for Thanksgiving dinner. After weeks of British supermarkets, it was glorious. The whipped cream and the eggnog, the canned pumpkin and the butter, but, most importantly, all the fresh vegetables. Piles of sweet potatoes and corn and carrots. All this fresh produce that apparently British people just do without. We felt some deep reservoir of appreciation for our country, our stupid country, our hateful country, our beautiful country, our own country. We cooked for a few days, ignoring the occasional mouse poking its head out from under the stove. And we had a lovely Thanksgiving. Even in terrible times, there are good times too. Our lives don't follow epochs. We live messier, more idiosyncratic histories.

Meg

IN PARTICULARLY COLD WINTERS the Central and Northern Hudson River sometimes freezes across its span. It doesn't freeze every year, but it is capable of becoming enough of a solid breathless surface to trap oil freighters in its icy jaws. They send huge icebreaker ships up and down the river to stop this from happening. They need to keep the waterway a water way and not a natural ice rink because commercial freight really doesn't care about your winter bucolic ice-skating dreams. The icebreakers create floating ice chunks that bob and swirl as they become trapped in the current. The water is so dark and cold and fast and sharp. It's arresting to me as I watch it while waiting for the Amtrak to New York City from the Rhinecliff train station. Eventually a skittering behemoth screams into the station spraying snow across anything mesmerized enough to stand still. In 2016, Rhinecliff became my new train station, replacing the Graham Avenue L stop, as Rhinecliff was now nearest to our new home two hours north of New York City.

Joseph very much wanted to leave the city. I could have stayed in Brooklyn forever. I could stay in most places that I am uncomfortable forever. Change makes me more uncomfortable, terrified. I resist change. Joseph does not. When he is unhappy with something, he changes it. He sees no point in unnecessary discomfort. As a woman, unnecessary discomfort is my native tongue. For a while the central argument in our relationship was about where we would live. The Hudson River Valley was a compromise, one that we were each excited to make. I wanted to stay close to my family and close to the Neo-Futurists, and

Joseph desperately wanted to leave the city. He wanted to move to the West Coast. I really didn't want to leave my family or start over again careerwise. Did they even have scrappy black box theaters in LA? LA has TV and movies, which were not places I thought would be possible for me to work. Trying to find an artistic foothold in Los Angeles seemed insurmountable to me, LA being the city of actors who worked many hours and spent many thousands of dollars every day to have a body that didn't look like mine. The thought of moving to a place where a very specific appearance was a requisite for respect and success repulsed me. I thought that no matter what I did to my body it would never be enough for LA, and the stories I wanted to tell would find no audience because of the package they were presented in. I had thighs, stretch marks, batwing arms, and a lower tummy pouch. I had the audacity to have all of those and to be a woman. In New York City I owned all of those things. I connected with others because of those things. I made art that celebrated and encouraged conversation about those things. The only women who looked like me who were on TV were on the Food Network and over the age of forty. My limited view at the time was that Angelenos were mostly actors and creators who sought fame and fortune, oftentimes at the expense of experimentation and quality.

The few times I had been to LA, whenever I would walk into a shop or a restaurant, people would turn to see who I was, clock that I was not famous, and then return to the foods they were pushing around their plates. This also happened in its own way at what I like to call "fancy people parties," the backroom gatherings of semi-famous or famous people that I was now privy to due to the commercial success of *Night Vale*. I felt seriously out of place and unwelcome. LA felt like a full-time "fancy people party" to me, and I didn't feel like there was a place for me there. I had worked so hard to carve out a place for myself and my work in New York. I didn't believe in myself enough to do it again, all for the want of sunshine and good Mexican food. These were my arguments against LA.

So, we moved to the Hudson River Valley because we both liked the area, after many romantic weekends stolen away from the city to look at mountains, drink wine, and sit in bathtubs. It checked a lot of both of our boxes for what we wanted from a home, mine being proximity to New York City and his being the opposite while still keeping me in his life. The home we bought was big. Your money goes a long way when you are used to paying gentrified Brooklyn rent. Our mortgage was half of our previous rent, and the house was more than two times the square footage of our old place. We bought it thinking we would live there for a while and build our lives there. That we would grow into it.

Joseph picked the house out, and when I toured it, I didn't hate it. The thing I liked most about it was that Joseph was excited about it, after looking at a lot of houses and failing to agree on anything. The master bedroom has a view of the Catskills that is instantly centering. When I saw it, I knew we would be happy there in the quiet, beautiful woods.

For the first four months we lived there, I kept asking Joseph to take me home. The first few times it was cute, and then I think it started to bum him out, so I stopped and started making it a home. I picked paint colors, hung artwork, and fell into the K-hole that is online rug shopping. I started planning my kitchen renovations and fixing the weird design choices made by the previous owners. Why are there nine sconces in my bedroom along with eight overhead lights? What were they *doing* in there?

It was a slow settle in because I was leaving for at least one weekday and every weekend to perform with the Neo-Futurists. My three subway stops away from the theater had changed into a two-to-three-hour one-way commute. I would board the train for my Tuesday rehearsals with the Neo-Futurists, my plays to be pitched for the week tucked into my adult lady commuter bag, and I would be so sad. Sad that there was so much railway between me and the city where my artistic community dwelled. Sad that I would have to spend the night in a sterile midlevel hotel room alone. I was trying to have it all, a great life on the road paired with an easy home life and continued access to the artistic playground of the Neo-Futurists theater, and it made me sad. I was reminded every day of what I had given up and what I was missing being so far away. There was so much time alone staring from train car windows out to a gray river or out of the windows of the Holiday Inn on West Fifty-Seventh Street that reflected the TV's sad image of Guy Fieri (the lone business traveler's only true companion) back at me and my loneliness. Winter is a tough season to feel that unmoored longing that comes from a massive lifestyle shift. I advise a springtime overhaul, if you can swing it.

We planned a large 2016 tour for *Welcome to Night Vale*. We performed 57 shows around the world for almost 50,000 people, including our first trip to Australia and New Zealand where we hand-fed kangaroos and ate Tim Tams and occasionally did shows. It was a very lax schedule. The "no worries, mate" vibe of the Australians was startling at first for a taskmaster tour manager like myself, but after a few days of dinner breaks on the beach, I acquiesced. I was physically as far from home as I had ever been, which has a certain heaviness to it. The weight of it rising the farther you get across the globe. The weight is built from homesickness and joy and fear and gratitude and responsibility to do your best and responsibility to honor the distances you get to travel when those who came before you never got to go anywhere. Trips like that one were big for me, and having Joseph by my side to help bear the weight of it and share in all of its newness was essential. He was living his promise of our home being anywhere as long as we were together. That promise would be called upon so much this year.

I was offered a great opportunity in the fall to help my friends Kate Jones and Desiree Burch start a London chapter of the Neo-Futurists alongside *Night Vale* collaborators and friends Cecil Baldwin and Jeffrey Cranor. We all jumped at the offer to stay in the UK for another month after our monthlong *Night Vale* Europe tour. I applied for my absentee ballot and prepared for two months away from my newly forming home in the Hudson River Valley. Joseph generously offered to join me, and we were both excited about the opportunity to get to live in another city for a little bit and to enjoy the cultural comforts that come from big-city living. We also just really missed being able to have food delivered, ok?

We rented a small Airbnb down the road from the theater. It was the standard Airbnb with all the trappings: nothing functional to cook with, a weird bed, sandpaper bath towels, and that same sourced-from-the-sale-section-of-any-generic-housewares-store Audrey Hepburn *Breakfast at Tiffany's* print. It worked, and I've had way worse Airbnbs. This one was very clean, which is all I ever really want from a stranger's toilet. The location was choice, being just a short walk to the theater and an adorable double-decker bus ride to rehearsals at Kate's. Joseph and I did find ourselves feeling cramped after getting used to our 3,000-square-foot home with separate offices, a king bed, and no one but the occasional owl within shouting distance. With Joseph on a novel deadline and me starting a theater company, we were now both working nose to nose over a tiny kitchen table into our laptops all day and sleeping far cozier than we had since our Bedford Avenue shag palace.

Helping Des and Kate build the company was a blast. Those two women are absolute forces of brilliant humor, generosity, and drive. I love succeeding with them, and I love failing with them. It's marvelous that the show we make gives opportunity for both many times over the course of any given performance. We had a great time planning workshops, casting, and of course doing the show each week. We were welcomed to London by great audiences and many talented people who wanted to join the company.

I loved our theater. It was on the top floor of the Rosemary Branch pub, a cozy pub that served Sunday roast and allowed dogs. I didn't know this at the time, but it's highly common for there to be small theaters above pubs in the UK. This is a genius idea, so genius I could *almost* forgive them for calling last call at those pubs at 11 P.M. *Almost.*

As is the tradition of me helping start a Neo-Futurist company, I got a call with bad news from home. My family dog Madison had died. She had been sick for a few weeks but died suddenly with my family, again all but me, surrounding her. I loved that dog more than I loved most people in my life. Joseph will tell you that she was a bad dog because she was deeply spoiled and needy. To which I would respond that he was bad, spoiled, and needy, and that I loved the dog more than him. Which maybe wasn't all the way true, but I would never stand for an ill word to be uttered about this beautiful soul in the body of a Labrador retriever.

We got Madison when she was a puppy my senior year of high school. I used to drive her around in my jeep and show her off to all my friends and never put her down. She was really beautiful and she knew it. Her coat was almost white and she shed it for all the world to share. She would get the newspapers in the morning and knew the difference between the *New York Times* and the *Star Ledger*. Whenever I was sick, she would lie on top of me with all seventy pounds of her wobbly lab bits. I was wrecked when I heard the news of her loss and doubly wrecked by my repeated absences from my distraught family's side. I was a terrible daughter and a terrible dog boss.

And then it got worse. The bad thing happened. Joseph and I spent Election Day 2016 seeing a performance of *In the Heights*. I had never seen it before and loved it. It's a great American story about the triumphs and troubles of often-marginalized people. It felt fitting to see it on what would be the day America would elect its first woman president. During intermission I checked my phone and saw an email that my laptop, which I thought I had just ruined by spilling water all over, was not ruined at all. It could be fixed. I was stoked that my carelessness had not caused permanent damage. I also responded to a text of a picture of my mom voting in her pantsuit. Joseph came back from the bathroom and saw me beaming at my phone. He was like, "Did they just call it for Hillary?" and I said no, not yet, and told him about my laptop and showed him the picture of my mom. That moment of joy was the last one I would have for very long time.

We got home from the show, and I started looking for hotel rooms in DC for the inauguration. I really wanted to bring my mom to DC to see the first woman president sworn in. Joseph and I went to bed before any states had been called because of the time difference. We set our alarm for 3 A.M. so we could get up and watch the returns. We woke up to some weird things happening. It was not a Hillary slam dunk. She was losing states everyone assumed were in the bag. I felt sick to my stomach as I was texting with my mom. She said, "I just have the worst feeling about this." The *New York Times* meter started showing a high percentage chance of a Republican victory. Fivethirty eight.com was scrambling. Joseph and I started crying; we turned the TV off. We each took a Xanax and fell asleep holding hands. We woke up the next day around one in the afternoon. It was still true. It was still broken.

We had rehearsal the day after the bad thing happened, and we were all wrecked, each of us having spent the night drinking or drugging our way to sleep after the horrible world shift toward darkness. I luckily had Joseph with me. Jeffrey had to weather it alone in his sad Airbnb with only a purloined bottled of his host's bourbon to ease his pain. But we pitched our angry plays, rehearsed and prepared our weekly show, because that's what Neo-Futurists do. We perform the public service of creating art about the current world, so that a community can come together to better process and better understand the world and the people who live in it. It also helps us process because it feels good to cry, scream, and throw things with other people sometimes. I smashed an entire cake each night that weekend for a play and it felt amazing. The Brits were sympathetic, almost as upset as we were but even more terrified having been through the Brexit vote only a few months before. A wave of global toxicity was now crashing on all shores.

The Regent's Canal, specifically the section between the Haggerston Bridge and the Islington Tunnel, is a thin sliver of a canal below the grinding city streets of east London. It is lined at its sides by slippery cobblestones because everything in London is always a little bit damp except for when it's completely soaked. The canal is filled almost to capacity with long houseboats of varying quality, some of them almost posh and some of them a true testament to the sheer will of rust, history, and stiff upper lips. They burn wood for heat, and the air smells like campfire mixed with burning plastic to remind you that you are in fact in a world-power city and not some sort of backwoods country waterway. The water is shockingly still and shallow. It looks like dark green glass, almost like you could walk right across it. I would go for runs down it in the afternoons just to move my body a little bit and to get out of our stifling apartment in the dreary post-presidential election/post-Brexit/post-hope late fall. I would think about the icy river near my new home and miss it. I would come back to the apartment both chilly and sweaty, and find Joseph. I'd tell him I want to go home. And through the magic of who he is, we were home.

We got back to New York a few days before Thanksgiving. We went wild at the much-missed American grocery store and cooked a huge meal for my family. I was thankful for home, even when it betrays you and elects a fascist, or even when it's new and strange, or even when it pulls on your heart and reminds you how far away you truly are. I was thankful for all the things that home can mean, and lucky enough for me, it means Joseph.

2017

Joseph

ON THE LAST NIGHT of 2016, we had Meg's family up to our house to celebrate. It snowed, and the ice crackle on the ground made magic of the woods around us. On the last night of 2017, we had Meg's family up to our house to celebrate. It snowed and the trees hung heavy with their frozen burden. Between these two nights, there was an entire year of my life, and yet the two nights were remarkably similar, so much so that I had to track down dated photos to remember which details belonged to which evening.

In both cases we made cocktails and food. The cocktails came from a bar tucked along the wall in our dining room that has become a joyful hobby for me. My parents did not drink hard liquor, and so I grew up with no concept of a cocktail. The forest-floor bite of gin and the campfire heat of bourbon were a complete mystery to me, and as an adult at first I found these disgusting. Then I came to appreciate that a fancy cocktail is one of the few times, as an adult, in which we are encouraged to play. Here is this treat with layers of colors and some silly ornament hanging off the side, and the treat's only purpose is to taste interesting and make you feel a little to the left of yourself. Our area of the Hudson Valley is full of world-class liquor distillers. The children of moonshine makers, these are people who know their way around a distillery. Our bar is crowded with bottles made within a few miles of our house, and the excuse to mix and match these with bits of local herbs and produce is one of my favorite things about having guests.

Then there is the food. Meg comes from the Italian tradition that if guests are invited, then there must be food available for all of them plus ten more that might theoretically show up on late notice. For a crowd of, say, four, she will produce trays of food big enough to bathe in, not to mention boards of cheese and crackers and huge basins of snacks to make sure no one is hungry by the time dinner starts. It is an aggressive hospitality, a hospitality that will make certain you feel good, goddammit. My domain in our dinner parties is the dessert, for which I favor some mixture of fruit and pastry that comes out of the oven a molten mess of juices, served tempered with a cold scoop of vanilla ice cream. Food is a way we express love. I want to cook with you. I want to eat with you. I want to end this year, this horrible year, and start this next year, this difficult year, by sitting down with all of you and food.

The snow outside on both of these New Year's Eves reflected the moonlight so clearly that the night went nearly as bright as day. Standing out in our yard as the moon rose, it was possible to distinctly see the individual trees in the forest that grew a half mile behind our house. This miracle of light was unfamiliar to me, a child of Southern California, for whom seasons had always been only a matter of the calendar. When I first came to New York in 2008, I arrived with a single thin sweatshirt that had my college's name on it. The fierceness of even October wind astonished me. And now here we are on an upstate New Year's, and I am having to learn how to shovel snow off a driveway. The first time I do this, I curse myself for ever having come to this worst of coasts, where the weather is a literal physical labor.

But also, Meg and I love the woods and we love creatures, and the snow becomes a paper that all of the creatures write upon. As the sun sets on New Year's we can look out at the tiny footprints of a cat, and the clumsy hoofprints of deer, and the light sketching of birds as they land and take off. The nature outside of our window is a constant wonderful surprise for us. On the last night of 2016. On the last night of 2017. On both nights, the snow. On both nights, the cold. But inside, on both nights, Meg's trays of food, and me, rummaging around in our bar that is decorated with an antique taxidermied pheasant and shouting, "Can I make you a cocktail?"

On the last night of 2016, we went midnight sledding in our yard, skidding down the ice and sliding out into the field behind our house. Lying on our backs at the bottom of the hill, delaying for a little the slow trudge back up, we looked at a perfectly clear sky bursting with stars, and then, sweating into our winter clothes, we stumbled back up the hill. Meg's mother took a livestream of us for Facebook, and there the light reflecting off the snow didn't register, and so each of us in turn appears to be boarding a sled and then sliding silently off into the dark.

On the last night of 2017 we put sparklers in the snow, shooting fragments of light into the ice where they smoldered for a moment before disappearing, leaving only a freckle of water in their wake. It was so cold outside that we would poke our bodies out just long enough to watch the show, then tuck back into the house where it was warm. The next morning, the sparklers still stood, burnt and blackened, in the snow where we had left them.

On both of these New Year's Eves, the evening eventually slid to a gentle slowness. We put on the TV, something boring and familiar. Tried to stay awake long enough to see the New Year in. We have enough excitement on the road, in our jobs, in the day-to-day pressure of making this ridiculous way of living work, that on these nights of celebration what we want is only peace at last. A year later my mother would visit on one of these upstate New Year's Eves, because the sledding and the snow and the food made it look so fun. That year it wouldn't snow, and she would be disappointed about the stillness of the later evening. "I sort of thought there would be more of a party," she said. But no; instead one of us will say, "Oh, it was midnight five minutes ago," and we'll congratulate ourselves on finally being allowed to go to bed.

Between those two quiet New Year's Eves, so much happened that looking back through my social media to jog my memory will be a series of surprises that all of this could fit into a single year. The more

I age, the more my memory is a flat surface. I know everything that happened, but there is no depth to it. I can't remember what happened which year, which events were near each other. My memories are less like a movie and more like a mural, full of detail, but ultimately not useful as a timeline.

This was the year our third nephew was born, the first on Meg's side. This was the year we founded a podcast convention, because most podcast conventions up to that point had either been business conferences or stand-up comedy festivals. We wanted something that was for fans of podcasts by fans of podcasts. And it was. Podcon was beautiful, right up until it folded two years later because it never made money and everyone involved in organizing it had twenty other jobs.

This was the year I went on a book tour, 27 cities in 32 days, and also Meg and I toured the world again with the *Night Vale* live show. This was the year when touring stopped feeling like a grand adventure and became what it was: our job. Touring shifted from our future to our present, and that raised the question for us: Ok, if this isn't our future anymore, then what is?

This was the year I ran out of road trip material for my road trip fiction podcast *Alice Isn't Dead*, so I rented a car in Los Angeles and took off east to the desert for a week. I drove to the shantytowns of Slab City, near the dead Salton Sea, where one of the hand-built shacks I drove by had a *Night Vale* logo spray painted on the side. I drove to Death Valley and slept the night in a haunted opera house that used to be a borax mine. And I got what I wanted, which was material to write about. Here I am writing about it again.

This was the year we went dogsledding on the frozen Mirror Lake with Meg's family in upstate New York. It was the year I started a podcast I had dreamed about making for a long time, in which I interviewed one of my favorite musicians in his basement, going song by song through one of his albums, sitting cross-legged on an old mattress as the pipes hummed from someone washing the dishes upstairs.

It was a year like every year since this stupid lottery win that was *Night Vale*'s success. It was hectic and stressful and I wouldn't trade it for anything and god I wish we got more sleep. But it started and ended the way Meg and I like it: quietly.

On the first day of 2017, as I do on most first days of most years, I woke up hungover. My body won't even offer the comfort of consistency. Sometimes I'll drink until I'm woozy and feel fine the next day. Other times I'll drink half a beer and walk around groaning the next day, one hand on my churning stomach. This time I definitely felt it. I made cinnamon rolls, as I do every New Year's morning. I make way too much, more than all of us could possibly eat. I learned that kind of hospitality from Meg. We put on the Rose Parade. We sit on the couch. And we lean into each other. As we do every day we can. As we'll keep doing until we can't anymore.

We start every year the way we want to live it. Together, and eating.

Meg

IN EARLY 2017 I spent six hours and almost $500 getting my dark red hair bleached to blond. Up until this point, I had lived my life as some form of redhead. I went to a fancy salon on Fifth Avenue where it was rumored that Beyoncé once had her extensions dyed. I booked the appointment on impulse and arrived hungover after a night of post-Neo-Futurist-show drinking. I almost passed out in the salon chair under the heat lamp from my hangover nausea coupled with the extreme pain of bleach burning through my scalp. Welcome to 2017, a year of change and chemical burns.

The world felt horrifyingly out of control after the 2016 election. I white-knuckled onto any semblance of power that remained. I latched onto the control over the way my life looked and the way I looked in it. All my big plans for my future were now threatened by the uncertainty of old white madmen and their dangerous ideas. I felt like we were running out of time to experience all the experiences our place in time had to offer. The clock was ticking down on my chance to swim in all the seas before they were poisoned, to travel to all of the countries before bans and border walls were built, and to finally live the dream of being a bottle blonde before I was grabbed by the pussy and thrown into a forced breeding pen. The world around us was changing fast and I wanted to prove I could change too. I could be in control of one goddamn thing. When I returned home from the salon I learned that Joseph didn't really dig the whole blonde thing and was very confused about where his frisky redhead had gone. But I was not yet legally required by the state to give a fuck about what my husband thinks about my hair.

There are the changes we choose and the changes we don't. Both terrify me. My brain is not afraid of change. My brain loves the challenge of finding routes on new pathways forming. But my brain is constantly being screamed at by my guts, "Don't trust the new thing! New thing bad!" My guts are afraid of change. They always have been. At eight years old I cried hysterically for several hours when my parents got a new couch. My best guess is that this fear stems from a lack of trust—trust in myself, trust in other people's will and their intentions, trust in the new couch to hold me as well as the old one had.

I trust in Joseph, most of the time, at least. He has a steady hand when it comes to change. He doesn't fear change, and he trusts that no matter what it is, it will work out. He packed up his whole life and moved to New York at twenty-two without knowing anyone there—in some sort of reverse *Fievel Goes West* leap of faith—Fink went east. It worked out for him. The tiny Jewish mouse finds a home in the end of both stories. Joseph's mentality is a very healthy counterbalance to my deeply passionate love of stasis. If it wasn't for him, I likely would still be living in my parents' house, chain-smoking, selling insurance, and box dying my hair red.

Joseph and I began to weather the serious political shift in our world. We chose to combat our terror with action, as many people did during this time. In addition to my deeply feminist statement of bodily autonomy by way of brave bleaching, we attended the Women's March in NYC in January. We arrived separately and couldn't find each other. I was in the city the night before performing, and Joseph took the train down to meet me. Cell phones stopped working, and it took hours for texts to go through. We eventually found each other after smushing past people and standing on our toes peering over crowds for hours. All for the opportunity to hold hands and walk up Fifth Avenue—to be there together in this mass of outrage, empowerment, and the terrible unknown.

We had a tiny taste of what the world would look like without phones to connect us, what it was like to be alone in masses of people and searching for each other. We were now on edge. In quite possibly the most bougie doomsday prepping, we started drinking all of our good wine because we were worried we would be blown up before we got a chance to drink it.

Later that year, I was in Helsinki on tour and Joseph was in LA for work. We realized that we were the farthest away from each other we had ever been and Trump's sticky ketchup-crusted finger was on the nuke button. We decided that our plan, if we needed it in case of global apocalypse, would be to meet back at our house, even if we had to walk there. We were just to wait at our meeting place and hope that the other person showed up—to trust that we could find each other. It's a laughably terrible plan that involved me having to wait for the Bering Strait to freeze to be able to walk across it, but I found comfort in believing that it was possible. That I could just walk back to my home from across the globe. This was a conversation we never thought we would need to have even a few months prior, but there we were: two naive kids warmly swaddled in that hopey-changey Obama-branded weighted blanket waking up on the hard cold dirty piss-dribbled bathroom floor of Trump's America and planning for the worst.

Joseph and I went to another protest in our tiny upstate town a few weeks after the Women's March. There were about eight people in attendance, and Trump supporters yelled at us as they drove by in their cars and trucks adorned with NRA and Hillary for Prison bumper stickers. We met another couple at the protest, and they asked us to join them for dinner. It was a really nice moment of connection in a place of disappointment and estrangement in our community. We talked about how there has always been a monster under the bed in America. We hoped that now more people would listen and believe the monster *is* really under there and that it's starting to get increasingly comfortable poking its terrifying hooded head out during the daytime. We never hung out with that couple again. We exchanged a few emails and then lost touch. It turned out to be just a one-night protest stand, but it impregnated us with the hope that new connections could be formed in this time of fear even if just for one magical night.

Change begets change. The major changes of the world ripple into smaller changes in our individual worlds. In January of 2017, the Neo-Futurists sought out change. The Chicago company lost the rights to our show's title *Too Much Light Makes the Baby Go Blind* due to a whole bunch of licensing bullshit that I'm not going to waste space with here. In solidarity, the New York and San Francisco companies did not renew their contracts for the name rights. Myself and several representatives from all three companies began the task of renaming the show and rethinking all of the aspects and attributes of the show, to only bring forward into the future what *we* wanted.

I was getting ready to move on from the Neo-Futurists when all of this happened, but this was an opportunity and an obligation that I couldn't turn my back on. The first few months of the year were filled with meetings, retreats, new ideas, and of course, shows. Because sometimes that toxic old adage "the show must go on" can feel like the most sacred prayer. We were renovating our show as we were performing it, and our audience got to watch—watch us fight to keep our lights on and not become just another cool East Village thing killed by The Man.

After one very good show in July, I felt a feeling of certainty come over me. "I can leave this here" is what I heard clearly from inside of myself. I was ready to move on. It was completely clear in my guts and my brain. I walked out of the theater that night and I knew it was the last show I would ever do as a permanent ensemble member. The bleach on my hair ate away my fear. I wasn't afraid of this change. I would still me be even if I wasn't a redhead, and I would still be me even if I wasn't a Neo-Futurist.

Unlike with my hair, Joseph was *very* supportive of my decision to move on from the Neo-Futurists. The partners of Neo-Futurists are referred to as "Neo-Widows" because being in that theater company takes a whole hell of a lot of your time. Joseph was ready for me to come home—to spend weekends together—to not hear me bitch about schedules and fellow ensemble members and the stresses of putting on a new show every week. Joseph knows that I am terrible with change and that I need to be coaxed toward it like you would coax a stubborn cat into a kitty carrier. He encouraged me to leave for years before I did, but just like the cat going into the carrier, it had to be my own idea.

With my role in the Neo-Futurists winding down, my role on the *Night Vale* team ramped up. For better or worse, Joseph found himself at the helm of a burgeoning media company, Night Vale Presents. We decided to branch out and form a podcast network with new podcasts by Joseph and Jeffrey and a number of other artists. I took on the role of tour director, handling all the things related to our live shows.

Night Vale's seemingly overnight success led to us needing to assemble the infrastructure of a legitimate business very rapidly. Everyone was truly trying their best to put banking, insurance, donations, merchandise, marketing, and touring practices and systems in place. But our best sometimes wasn't good enough. Big things took precedence over small things, but small things became big things when ignored.

When I would bring issues to Joseph's attention, we would often fight about them. He didn't like to hear at all hours of the day how we were failing. It was distracting to his writing and creative space for me to bust in randomly to complain that our health insurance hadn't been paid or that we hit our credit limit. I also sometimes just wanted to vent about my job because complaining is always one of my favorite topics of conversation. Joseph can't hear the venting and not see that it's something he needs to fix. It's a complicated place to be for all parties with lots of new territory to be mapped.

There's this really great thing that comes with living with a fellow artist. Especially one you are married to, because you generally think the world of them and are often within shouting distance of them, should you need to run something by them. There's this really terrible thing that comes with living with your boss. Especially one you are married to, because you generally think the world of them and are often within shouting distance of them, should you need to run something by them.

Working together as a couple is a gift and a challenge for us. It's nice to be able to have lunch with your husband every day. It's not nice to feel like you can never leave the office because the work conversations never stop. We learned to try to draw lines around when it's ok to talk about work and when it is not. We follow these rules sometimes to great success and break them to big blowout fights every so often. Usually these fights happen when I am doing laundry, because Joseph's office is adjacent to the laundry room and I pop in to move a load around, mention a problem I'm having in my workday, and then we end up screaming at each other for 45 minutes. If you thought laundry was your least favorite chore, now imagine having to do it in your grumpy boss's office that he doesn't want you in.

Working together and from home has so many benefits, all of which erode when your home is under renovation and subsequently so is your office. Disturbances in home life are the one type of change that Joseph does not do well with. If he thought me being blond was a tough pill to swallow, he was really gonna have some trouble with there being no first floor in our house for months. After so much touring, we both really thrive on the comfort of a domestic routine. So, when I decided to embark on a major kitchen renovation, I attempted to schedule it for when he would be away on book tour. I say attempted because trying to plan around the timetable of a contractor's alchemy is like trying to control the weather. Our contractor assured us that it could be done while Joseph was away for a month, which, of course, turns out was a fucking lie. I didn't vet the contractor well, that's on me. They had really good branding, and I am a sucker for packaging. Which is how you end up getting your scalp burned by the Beyoncé salon and your remodeling project months late and thousands over budget.

I went to go live with my parents while the house was under construction and Joseph was on tour. I found myself again back in my childhood bedroom, long since converted into a fashionable guest room. I myself had long since converted into a starkly different person from the last time I inhabited that space just five years ago. I was married. I owned a home. I had performed on many of the world's great and not-so-great stages. I hadn't smoked or done drugs in years, and I exercised every day with a blond ponytail swaying behind me. Everything had changed.

My sister, who lived nearby to my parents, changed the branches of our family tree by giving birth to my nephew. The day Joseph's book tour started was the day he was born. It was one of life's perfect timings, as I was now living just a short walk to my sister's house and there was a new baby in the family. I had missed so many important family events over the years because of touring and the time demands of my career, it was one of the highlights of my life to get to be there for this. I would walk over to my sister's house every morning like a Marilyn Monroe Mary Poppins with a bag full of lactation cookies and protein smoothies. And spend all day with our family's new addition, changing diapers, giving baths, and being with my sister on her new journey of motherhood. I loved getting to be there with my sister. She was exhausted but a total natural new mom who found fun in all that this new experience had to offer. We accidentally turned the baby blue once by putting him in a dark blue onesie with leaky dye after a bath. We kept just saying to each other "He's blue?" "He's fine." "Heeeeee's blue!" These moments are not worth trading for all the backstage snacks and spotlights in the world.

When Joseph returned from his book tour we went back to our house and found it nowhere near ready. After over a month of construction, the first floor was mostly plaster dust and ripped up drywall. We made a makeshift kitchen in the basement with a hot plate and a microwave, where I tried my best to make us edible food.

After one particularly long day, when I went to make dinner, I could not locate the can opener. I went upstairs to try and find it among our boxes of storage, and when I came back down, I found Joseph using the tip of my prized razor-sharp chef's knife and a hammer to chisel into the can. I lost my damn mind. If you are a cook you understand why. If you are not a cook let me try to explain to you why this turned my brain into fresh-out-of-the-microwave molten Hot Pockets filling. Think of your most valued item that you use every day; maybe it's your car or your phone or your wedding ring. Now imagine someone using that item and a hammer to chisel into a can of beans. Now imagine you have a hot-blooded Italian temper, have had a house full of construction dudes for weeks with no end in sight, and haven't eaten a fresh vegetable in months. Also remember you are never really fighting about the can of beans but instead fighting about every decision both of you have made to get to this specific moment in time wherein you are watching your beloved stabbing said beans in the dusty basement of what used to be your comforting home sweet home but is now just a hazardous shack of early morning buzz saws and way-too-expensive faucets in unopened boxes on the floor. Got it? Ok, good.

I said things I'm not proud of, reader. Dark things. We screamed at each other for a long time, then he left and went to the local diner alone. I used a screwdriver to get into the can of divorce beans and cried for an hour and a half. Joseph came home with a new can opener, the olive branch of our kitchen-renovation breaking-point battle royale.

The kitchen was eventually finished, although not actually so. I gave up and left a few things unfinished, because if the construction crew stayed a moment longer, Joseph was going to leave. And I would have no one to cook for in my Barbie Dream Kitchen complete with a six-burner stove, double oven, industrial vent hood, and expensive faucets that actually don't really work all that great.

The bleach ruined my fucking hair. A lot of it fell out and it won't grow long anymore and Joseph hated it. But I kept bleaching it and he kept loving me just the same. It made people who look at me every day look at me again and see that I was capable of transformation—that I still had power over my body. I needed to be seen that way in that moment. I needed to see myself that way, as a person who is afraid but can still author her own change.

They say if you can get through a major home renovation, your marriage is strong. They say if you can work with your partner, your marriage is strong. They say if you are attracted to your partner no matter what they happen to look like, then your marriage is strong. What they are really saying is if you and your partner can adapt to change together, global change, physical change, power dynamic change, then your relationship is strong. Your relationship is strong because it can change without breaking. Our relationship, while continually tested by my temper, his stubbornness, and the shifting world we live in, remains strong. Strength that is fueled by surviving missing can openers, shared offices, apocalypse planning, and even sudden impulse blondness.

2018

Joseph

UPSTATE NEW YORK HAD always been a compromise for us. I wanted to get away from New York City. Meg wanted to stay near it. And like any compromise, upstate didn't fit either of our needs exactly. Living in a rural area where we didn't know anyone wasn't easy, and trying to build a community of friends from scratch in a rural area wasn't easy either. So what happened was we retreated into ourselves. Our life was our house, and the farm stands near us, and the farm roads we ran along as dogs chased after us because people in rural areas don't tie up or fence their dogs at all and so those dogs chase anyone who runs by. Eventually the dogs would get to know us and would stop chasing us, glancing up from their naps and cocking their ears before going back to sleep.

It was lovely at times, life in the woods, but it was also isolating, and it was lonely. Especially when I stopped going on most of the *Night Vale* tours, because my physical presence wasn't necessary for them and I had too much writing work at home that needed to get done. Meg would venture out into the world, and I would stay, alone in the woods. I would cook dinner. I would watch TV. I would go weeks without talking in person to anyone at all. It drove me into myself in a way that I didn't like.

Which is when we started talking about California. It's where I grew up, and I've always wanted us to live there. My plan when I had moved to New York had been to live on the East Coast for an absolute maximum of five years before moving back, and at this point I was five years overdue.

So we decided to give living in Los Angeles part of the year a try. We were able to work from anywhere, and the slow development of television adaptations for two of my podcasts gave me some plausible reason why I should be in LA anyway, even if television is mostly waiting for an email letting you know that your show is the best work of art we've ever seen, possibly the best work in human history, but also sorry we have no interest in making it, thanks!

The Airbnb we stayed at in Los Angeles was a guesthouse in the neighborhood of Atwater Village, about as far from the ocean as you can get and still be in city limits. The guesthouse was in the back of a yard in which four goats lived. The goats were kept as pets by the family who lived there. They were fun to watch from the windows, although one of them had a tendency to ram anyone who entered the yard, and the little bastard knew to aim for the knees, so it was better to watch from afar.

The place didn't have much in the way of air conditioning, so when it got hot we opened all the windows, including those overlooking the goat pen. The goats were curious about us and would come to look at us with their cute devil eyes, sometimes propping themselves up on the windowsill to see better. I suppose it should not have been a surprise, then, when one of them leapt up over the sill and into the house. Suddenly we had a goat running around our living room. Meg grabbed it by the horns and dragged it back outside. After that, we left the windows overlooking the goat pen closed.

The other creature of note at this rental was a gray cat who would whine to come in at every opportunity. She didn't have a collar, and I didn't know if she was a stray cat or what. The first time she dropped by, I was worried she was hungry, and so I put some popcorn and beef jerky on the ground, to see if she would like either of those. Thus, I earned her eternal friendship. She would come in through the window, hang out on our couch, even let us pick her up, and then, after visiting for a bit, she would hop back out the window. We named her

Barbara Emmaline Quendeline Sauce, or Barb E. Q. Sauce for short. Later we found out that she belonged to the family who owned the goats, and that she was a male cat they had named Creed. But to us, she would only ever be our Barb E. Q. Sauce.

"What do you think she's thinking about?" I would say, as Barbara curled up purring on my lap.

"Murder," Meg would say fondly and give her a soft pat on the head, which she could only do sparingly because she is very allergic to cats.

Coming to LA was intoxicating after our life in the woods. Our friends all lived a few minutes away. My family lived in the area too. My father grew up in Arcadia, twenty minutes east of our goat guesthouse, and my grandmother grew up in Edendale, a defunct town that used to exist just across the LA river. I was now a third-generation resident of this part of the city. But most important of all, restaurants would deliver to us. The first time I ordered a food delivery and it actually arrived, I felt like I had gotten away with a crime, and that soon I would be arrested for having it too good, and the subsequent jail time would be worth it.

We had friends over for parties, we had friends over for dinner, we had friends over for any reason at all, eating in the warm outdoors that is possible in Southern California even in winter. We saw theater, and concerts. The two of us were gluttons for big-city life after our time upstate. I knew that I couldn't go back to just living in the woods all the time. And that was the problem.

Because we owned a house in the woods. We had filled it with furniture. We had built a life there, even if it was a life neither of us was entirely satisfied with. Our years of touring had given us a desire for a quiet center. But what to do now that we realized that maybe we had invested it all into settling down in a place neither of us really wanted to settle down? How do we even start to think about the possibility that we had made a mistake that big? So we didn't think about it. We lived in LA for a few months, and then we went back to New York and didn't talk about what to do next.

That fall I went on my fourth book tour. It should have been routine at that point. It felt like book tours were a skill I had truly gotten a handle on. But this tour would make me reconsider everything about how I was choosing to live.

It started out fine. Meg was going to accompany me for the first four stops, so she drove and I picked out podcasts to listen to. We made plans to have dinner with a friend in Chicago, and then the next day to get tattoos from an artist there whose work we liked. *This is almost a vacation instead of work*, I thought. I woke up the third morning of the tour with a terrible sinus infection. This is not unusual for me. I spent most of my childhood getting three or four sinus infections a year until I found out as an adult that I have allergies and I need to take allergy pills. Still, I know the course of a sinus infection, and I can deal with it.

The drive to Lexington that day took nine hours over winding passes through the Smoky Mountains. It poured the entire time, rain so hard that the windshield wipers couldn't keep up. My stomach started to hurt, and I was having trouble breathing. The next day we went to the Lexington Horse Park so Meg could meet the horses. I felt awful and spent a lot of our time sitting on benches trying to will myself back into optimism.

By the time we got to Chicago, my nose had fully sealed. We had dinner with our friend at a restaurant run by a *Top Chef* winner that we had wanted to try for years. I could not taste a thing. I could feel myself becoming frustrated and sad, and I still felt awful from the infection. On the twenty-minute drive home—and I apologize for being blunt, but this detail became a big part of my life over these few weeks—I abruptly became certain I was going to shit myself. I spent the entire night back and forth to the bathroom, never relieving the pain in my guts.

The next day we got our tattoos. As Meg got hers, I excused myself to the parlor's bathroom and threw up. My stomach heaved with painful contractions. I knew I wasn't going to be able to do the reading that night. For the first time ever, I had to cancel an event. It felt terrible, but I didn't see any way I was going to be able to get myself all the way across the city and through ninety minutes of event in the condition I was in. So now I was sick and feeling guilty about letting down the people who had bought tickets, and this made me depressed and anxious.

With Meg's support, I managed to make it to the next event in Ann Arbor and get through it, although I had a full panic attack onstage. I don't think anyone noticed. Having anxiety makes a person a wonderful performer, maintaining a placid face while the brain melts into formless fear.

The day after that, Meg had to go home, and I went on alone. Without Meg's help, my anxiety consumed me. A book tour, despite one spending each event talking and talking, is a truly solitary experience, and I was not good company for myself at the time. My lowest point came on the forty-five-minute flight from LA to San Francisco, a flight I spent the better of on my knees in the tiny airplane's bathroom, dry heaving and dry heaving and not understanding what was happening to me.

Here's what was happening to me. My years of anxiety and touring had caught up. And I had given myself IBS through sheer stress. Now when I get anxious, which is a lot of the time, I get nauseous. I feel like I need to throw up, but if I try, I only dry heave. My body falls apart when my mind does. And I knew then, with a dreadful certainty, that the life of a touring artist was not one I could live anymore. It was over for me. My own bodily functions had rebelled and told me to finally come home. But where was home?

I love summers in the Hudson River Valley, when every plant bursts lush and green and the skies are heavy with water. I love the farm stand near our house, piled high with peaches in July and tomatoes in August and thirty different kinds of apples in September, each variety with a lovingly written placard giving a history of the type and its best uses in the kitchen. I love going for runs upstate, where a passing car is a rarity and the Catskills reveal themselves when the trees open up to the view.

But I love winters in California, when every plant bursts lush and green on the little bit of rain that hits the state. I love the smell of Los Angeles—herbs and warm dirt. I love our farmers' market that is piled with produce year-round, not only in the four-month harvest season of upstate. I love the food in Los Angeles. I love that I can see world-class theater a short drive from my house, but still live in a quiet neighborhood. I love having spur-of-the-moment lunches with friends.

I love my house in the Hudson River Valley. I love having my own office, even if it is just our basement. I love my desk there. I love our porch and the rocking chairs on our porch and the view of the woods from our porch. I love our kitchen, how we have changed it to fit exactly what we want from it. I love living on a road so quiet that every car passing by is an event and we look up to think, *Who is that and why are they driving by our house?* I love nights upstate, the absolute silence and the absolute dark.

But I love my neighborhood in California. The architecture, which is far more varied and beautiful than the utilitarian homes of the Northeast. I love the people, who come from different backgrounds and all live such different lives compared to the homogeny of rural New York. I love the simplicity of our life in LA, without all the stuff we've bogged ourselves down with over the years. I love never having to worry that our pipes will freeze or that our propane will run out. I love living in a place where the weather is a mild curiosity and not a possible emergency.

I love both places, I do. And to love two places is to live always in longing for the other.

I want to live in California, but I also want to live in our house in New York. After our years of touring, we struggle to have the feeling that we belong anywhere at all. We've lived in our New York house for five years, but cumulatively have been gone on the road for likely two years of that. And Los Angeles has been immediately welcoming, but also everything about our life here feels provisional and temporary.

I don't know where home will end up for us. Even writing this now, a couple of years later, the decision is still in the air. We keep putting it off. And so we depend more and more on the sense of home that we had come to during that first year of touring. Wherever we both are, that is our home. Our bones and our skin, our muscles and our beating hearts, those have to serve as a sense of home, as we bounce back and forth across the country thinking, *I don't know, I just don't know, we'll decide next year, next year we'll decide.*

Meg

MY LIFE HAS HAD many exceptional days. In February of 2018 I performed *Welcome to Night Vale* live on the stage of the Sydney Opera House for a lovely audience that included both my parents, Joseph's mom, and my dear lifelong family friends who traveled halfway around the world just to be there. I am incredibly lucky and incredibly proud of the life we have built. But some of this wild life is filled with fantastically ordinary days—days filled with well-worn routines and the kinds of strange habits that are formed by sharing a home with someone for many years. In 2018 my normal days looked like this . . .

I wake up in my bedroom in our home in the Hudson River Valley. I pull my sleep mask from my eyes, and I can see the Catskill Mountains from my bed on a clear day. We don't have drapes on our windows because there is no one to see us but the mountains and the occasional lucky dog walker. Joseph is next to me, likely already awake and reading or checking his phone. I mumble, "Good morfing, baby" to him; my night guard muffles my words. I wear a night guard when I sleep that I call my muzzle. I grind my teeth so badly that I have given myself TMJ and ripped through the enamel on most of my molars. The stress of my incredible life isn't always pretty.

Sometimes I laugh in my sleep, so I'm told by Joseph. Joseph occasionally says very adorable things as he sleeps, "I am now accepting petting" being the cutest one to date. Though I rarely see Joseph sleep. I am the first one down and the last one up. I'm great at sleeping. If there were a sleep Olympics, I could be a contender.

Next, I get up and walk across the bedroom to the bathroom to pee and take out my mouth guard. Then I promptly get back in bed to check my emails and do the news and social media roundup. This is a terrible habit because starting the morning off with urgent emails heightens my stress level for the day but it also makes it so I can stay in bed longer before heading down to work. I trade the stress for the warmth of my flannel sheets with cartoon rabbits on them.

During this early morning phone deep dive, Joseph will bring me a coffee that he expertly prepared downstairs—the sounds of the preparation from the kitchen scoring my email reading and subsequent rage phone typing. Soon I hear his stompy feet pound up the stairs. He is remarkably heavy-footed for his size. It sounds like an unsteady manatee in tap shoes when he moves about the house. He pauses at the doorway in his robe, cup of coffee in his hand, and he whistles at me, then I meow back at him as a response, then he brings the coffee to me. I say thank you, he sits down on my side of the bed, watches me take my first sip, and then heads back downstairs. I enjoy my coffee in bed as I read and prepare for the day. This is an excellent way to wake up, one that I never thought possible when I was selling insurance by day, eating cigarettes for breakfast, and making theater until late in the night.

Eventually I put on my workout clothes and head downstairs to the kitchen. I pass Joseph in his chair in the living room with his feet up on our footstool that is shaped like a small black bear. Our house has a lot of weird shit in it, which should be no surprise given that we are weird people.

I walk to my stupidly expensive Vitamix blender. I will justify its ridiculous expense by saying that I've used it every day I've been home since 2014. I also have gotten smoothie on the ceiling of every home I've lived in since 2014. I love it and would like it to be my cremation urn. (As I carried it out of the store on the day I bought it, a car stopped to let me cross the street, and the passenger shouted out their window, "Congratulations on your Vitamix." It was so nice to have their blessing.) I make a smoothie for both of us (recipe follows). This fucking epic blender could liquidate a cinder block. It is Very. Fucking. Loud. I pour one smoothie for Joseph and one for myself in our dark purple four-cup mason jars that I bought at Target. I take the chipped one because I use a metal straw and Joseph doesn't like metal straws. I won't let him use the plastic ones because of the sea turtles, so he has to have the unbroken cup to avoid injury to his perfect slutty little mouth. I deliver Joseph the smoothie either to his chair or down to his office. I hand it to him and say, "Here is your wet food" or "Enjoy your cold fruit soup."

Then I bring my smoothie to my office, where I resume work. I tackle the morning's work projects from my office that overlooks our backyard where I occasionally see deer. Joseph and I named the deer in our yard Shamrock and Angela. If I see them, I will Google-chat to let Joseph know they are out. Or sometimes I just scream, "Shamrock!" "Angela!" "You are deer!" at them very loudly until they look back at me. Then we stare at each other until one of us moves on with our day. Usually it's the deer that move first.

Late morning, I go for a run, and before I leave I yell down to Joseph's office, "I do my runs!" This way he knows I'm gone in case I don't come back because I have been murdered by one of the backwoods folk, joined the pack of deer, or (more likely) have fallen down.

I go for a nice long run on the mostly abandoned country roads that surround our house. It's very hilly, and if it's not raining or snowing I get out there whether it is 20 degrees or 90 degrees. I run very slowly, so slowly that when the rare stranger sees me, they cheer me on like it's my first day off the couch. I've asked Joseph if many strangers cheer him on when he's out running, and he says they do not. People love to applaud a fat woman exercising. They're like, "Keep it up!" and

I want to turn to them and say, "Bitch, I've been running fifteen to twenty-five miles a week for the past five years. I have kept it up, now please stop talking to me before I fuck you up."

I love running, and I have not gotten one second faster at it since I started in 2014. I can just run a lot farther now. I'm far too pear-shaped to make sense as a runner. I'm Italian American, I'm built to feed, not built for speed. All of my weight is in my thighs, hips, and ass and everything jiggles like lasagna in an earthquake. But I still do it. It's nice to get outside and to tire out my legs and my mind.

I have no plan or desire to train for any sort of race. Getting better at hobbies is not something I really prioritize, as I don't want my obsessively organized brain to strangle everything I love about them. I put so much pressure on trying to be excellent as a tour manager, writer, and performer that I give myself a break on the stuff that doesn't pay the bills. It feels great to be bad at something and have there be no consequences other than well-meaning fat-phobic strangers getting all cheering section on me as I slowly heave my oversize pelvis up a hill.

When I return from my run, it's time for lunch or, as Joseph and I call it, "hashtag lunch." There are a number of things that we eat for lunch. Joseph often eats leftovers from dinner the night before. I usually engage in some sort of almond butter and apple situation. We watch a TV show over lunch, one of the reality shows we enjoy together (these are different from the reality shows I enjoy alone that are full trash). We watch competition shows like *Top Chef*, *American Ninja Warrior*, *The Great British Baking Show*, or *The Amazing Race*. We fantasize about being on *The Amazing Race*. Even though our lives *are* the Amazing fucking Race, we just would like the chance to show the world how good we are at airports and that one competitive-eating challenge they have each season.

After lunch it's back to work for as long as I can stand it. I spend hours poring over the small details of our tours, like how many size-small T-shirts should I order for the Denver show. And big details like can we afford to do an Australia tour, or will the conversion rate put us in the red? And do we have the right insurance if I kill someone with a van? I really love arts management and really love working for a startup, but it is a lot. It takes up most of the space in my life. My brain is constantly working away at problems even as I sleep and bite through my mouth guard.

Part of my job is "awfulizing," or determining what the worst thing that could happen to us is and figuring how to prevent it and in the absence of prevention planning for the awful. Some of this awfulizing is necessary because we need plans in place if we have to miss a show due to weather or sickness. Some of it is just my terrible brain at work. My brain wants to solve the problem before it happens because then it will make the awfulness of the problem less awful. It wants to find a way to control the out of control. The stakes are high. I am in charge of this precious thing that is very important to many people worldwide and is responsible for both my family's livelihood and my closest friends' livelihoods. Every day, I try to be worthy of being entrusted with this responsibility by being two steps ahead of the snowball rolling down the hill at us. I used to get high from drugs and bingeing. Now, I get a huge rush when I can solve a problem before it becomes one. I will always find a way.

On Wednesdays during the growing season I go to the farm stand in the late afternoon. I meticulously menu plan our week based on what I can get at the market. The market has a flow to it. We start the season with blueberries and greens, and then the peaches and corn come up. Next it's months of tomatoes of all shapes and sizes. Then we hit autumn, which is the most bountiful time in the Hudson River Valley with tons of squash and most notably dozens of varieties of apples. So many apples that we call the market the Apple Store.

For the first quarter of my life I didn't know how to feed myself.

Food is a deeply confusing daily activity for someone with eating disorders. When you use food as a drug it's really tough to learn to use it as nourishment. Years of dieting, tracking, fasting, and bingeing have hardwired my brain so that food is often all I can think about. What can I eat? When and how much can I eat? Am I eating more than these other people eating with me? Why do I feel so good when my stomach is painfully empty? Why do I feel nothing at all when I'm bingeing? Learning more about cooking—the techniques along with the cultural, the historical, the environmental, and the economic aspects of food—has really helped in my healing. It allows me to academize my obsession with food and enables food to be in my life without weaponizing it against myself. Instead of thinking harmful thoughts about food, I'm thinking about the implications of global climate change on coffee production or about whether I'm ready yet for my own sourdough starter (I'm not).

After I leave the Apple Store, I go to the supermarket to get all the nonproduce things we need. I have a love/hate relationship with our local grocery store. I can never count on them to have that one random bougie-ass item I need like dried porcini mushrooms or soba noodles or sun-dried tomatoes, and their bulk section always looks like a team of horses got loose, took horse-size bong rips, and went to town on it.

I also love it because I love food, and at grocery stores food is celebrated. The employees are friendly and skew toward the goth teenager demographic (my personal favorite model of teen). There are several cartoonishly large cans of baked beans that no one ever buys that fascinate me. People have taken to writing messages to each other in the dust that collects on the top of the cans, which creates this trail log for the canned-vegetable aisle.

I head home from the store and call my mom or my sister on the drive just to see what they are up to and how their days are going. I pull into our driveway, and Joseph will sometimes pop out to help me with the bags and sometimes not. I will be grumpy and resentful if he doesn't.

I make us dinner, which is usually some big pile of vegetables. When dinner is ready, I'll stand at the top of the stairs and yell down to his office, "Oh, Bear!" I do a lot of yelling down or up stairs. Again, I'm Italian American, we yell in the home. Joseph will come upstairs and say, "It looks wonderful, thank you, Bear." We eat in our kitchen while watching TV. If we have kids, we will have to stop doing this because it apparently makes their brains garbage and gets them hooked on opiates, but we enjoy it while we can. I grew up watching TV at the dinner table and I can confirm my brain is garbage, but I have seen every episode of *Frasier*, so there's that.

Joseph and I both feel as though the day is incomplete without dessert. Frequently we have frozen Greek yogurt pops that I buy in the "Novelty" section of our grocery store, which sounds vaguely pornographic but mostly just contains ice pops, which *are* dick shaped, so there you go. Other nights we have what has been one of Joseph's great culinary contributions to our relationship, a dish which he has named the McFlurry after the McDonald's dessert, which he has never actually eaten (recipe follows).

On Friday nights we will do shabbat dinner. After leaving the Neo-Futurists, for the first time in ten years I have my Friday nights free, no longer schlepping bags of props on the subway and panic eating a dollar slice on my way to rehearsal. I now spend my Fridays roasting chicken and braiding challah (recipe follows) like a shiksa with something to prove. Because I am a shiksa with something to prove. I have no desire to convert to Judaism, but I love the traditions and celebrations that Joseph and his family have shared with me. Specifically, the food ones.

After dinner Joseph and I snuggle on the chaise lounge section of our couch under a queen-size comforter from my freshman year dorm bed, and we watch more TV. Usually we watch an hourlong show or a movie. We've watched the entirety of *The Wire* and *Treme*, twice.

Then we head up to our bedroom. I take a shower before bed because I am always freezing cold, so I need to parboil myself before attempting to sleep in our freezing bedroom. Joseph runs hot and is covered in a thick coat of hair, so we keep our bedroom like a fur cold-storage unit. We both read before bed. I like nonfiction, memoir, and food magazines, and he likes fiction. I usually fall asleep by dropping the book on my face. I take off my glasses, turn out my light, put on my sleep mask and muzzle, and say "Goofnight, babe. I luff you. I'll see you in Dreamland." Then there is a short jokey discussion about where in Dreamland we will meet tonight. "Snoozleton?" "North Snoozleton?" "Pillow Falls?" Then I go to sleep where I will stay uninterrupted for nine glorious hours. Until, with any luck, it all happens again.

Congratulations on Your Vitamix Smoothie

2 cups unsweetened vanilla almond milk
1 cup nonfat Greek yogurt
2 large handfuls of baby spinach
1 tablespoon peanut butter
1 frozen banana
$1/2$ cup each frozen cherries, strawberries, and blueberries

Serves 2

Place all the ingredients into your high-powered blender that costs more than your first car and has similar horsepower. Watch as solid becomes liquid and marvel at man's triumph over the need to chew. I like mine so thick my sinus cavities collapse as I pull it through the straw. Blend yours until the desired consistency. Makes a fuck ton, you won't need to eat until lunch.

Joseph Fink Has Never Had a Real McFlurry

2 scoops of the frozen dessert product of your choice. Joseph
   recommends Ben & Jerry's Cherry Garcia low-fat frozen yogurt.
1 handful of Wheat Chex cereal
1 to 2 splashes of a milk of your choice
1 tablespoon chocolate chips (optional)

Serves 1

Add all the ingredients to a coffee mug. Wait as much
time as your patience will allow for the frozen parts to soften
(my record is thirty seconds), stir, and enjoy.

Manic Pixie Dream Shiksa Challah

2 teaspoons active dry yeast
1 cup warm water
$1/4$ cup plus 2 teaspoons honey
2 tablespoons melted butter
2 large eggs
2 tablespoons chopped fresh rosemary
2 teaspoons salt
zest of one large lemon
1 cup whole wheat flour
2 cups white flour, divided
$1/4$ cup sesame seeds
sprinkle of flaky sea salt (optional)

*Serves 6 at a polite dinner party, serves 2 where manners don't
matter*

Dissolve the yeast in warm water in a large mixing bowl. Add two teaspoons of the honey and let the mixture sit for five minutes until the yeast has bloomed. Add the slightly cooled melted butter, the remaining honey, one egg, rosemary, salt, and lemon zest and stir to combine. Add the whole wheat and white flours $1/2$ cup at a time and stir between additions to incorporate until a wet dough has been formed. You may not need all the flour or you may need more. Maybe I would know exactly how much you would need if I was one of the chosen people, but I am not.

Sprinkle a clean countertop or cutting board with flour and knead the dough, adding more flour as needed to stop sticking, until the dough bounces back when poked, 5 to 7 minutes of consistent kneading. I like to stare off into the distance as I knead and think of all the women who came before me who made this bread each week. And how even some of them, like me, were dressed up as a bride at eight years old, married to Jesus, and fed his body in the form of crackers by a man wearing a gilded bathrobe.

Form the dough into a ball. Place the dough ball back into the mixing bowl, cover with a clean dishcloth, and place the dough somewhere warm for at least 1 hour, or until it has doubled in size. In my house, our bedroom gets warm in the later afternoon, so I like to proof my dough up there. We call it the Master Breadroom.

After the dough has risen, give it a light punch down and turn it out of the bowl back onto the floured surface. Divide the dough into four equal ropes and braid them together, one rope over each, until a loaf has been formed. Or watch a couple videos of challah braiding on YouTube and get flour all over your phone for inspiration.

Place the loaf on a parchment-lined baking sheet and cover with a clean dishcloth and let rest for 15 minutes. Preheat the oven to 375 degrees. Beat the remaining egg in a small bowl and brush it onto the loaf. Sprinkle the sesame seeds and flaky sea salt over the loaf. Bake for 25 to 35 minutes, rotating once. Your oven is not my oven. We all have different experiences and lives that lead us to this very moment. Don't burn the bread. It's done when it's golden and smells so good that you will have a hard think about how you were taught that some shitty-ass dry cracker was god, when obviously god is right before you and it is something that you made with your own hands. Serve right from the oven with butter. Learn the blessing for bread that you say before you eat it from your patient spouse who married you even though their grandma gave them shit about it.

2019

Joseph

OUR TIME IN LA had gone well enough that we decided to do the same again the next year. We showed up at our goat Airbnb to discover that the owners had since started a massive construction project. Jackhammers in the morning. Nail guns in the evening. A muralist whose "process" involved blaring a Maroon 5 song on loop for six to seven hours. As cute as the goats were (still very cute), it was an intolerable situation. So just as our Brooklyn landlord's renovation in 2015 had caused us to impulse buy a house upstate, we once again made a major life decision just to get out away from annoying construction noise.

That week we went and rented a house in the same neighborhood. Full-time, year-round rented. We now had our own place in LA. And since we had a place in LA and renting a car for long periods is absurdly expensive, we also went ahead and bought a car there. Suddenly we were no longer on a lark, spending a couple of months on the West Coast to see if we liked it. We now had full-time homes on both coasts and had invested enough in this one to commit to spending half the year there. But it got us away from that fucking Maroon 5–inspired muralist, so that worked.

We would miss Barb E. Q. Sauce, but as it happened the new house came with a cat of its own. A feral cat who lived in the backyard and who the landlord called "Kitty," but, as is our tradition, we renamed to "Miss Fancy Feast." Every morning and evening we feed her, and she sits at the edge of the patio and shouts at us while we do it. Reluctantly, we have come to the conclusion that she is "adorable" and "our little cat," which has been a difficult reality to face for both of us.

When I realized I probably needed serious help with my mental situation was when I got rabies. Very few people survive rabies. In fact, there has only been one case that I could find online of someone developing rabies and surviving the experience. I suppose, then, that I would be the second.

How it happened was I startled Fancy Feast while I was feeding her and she lightly scratched me on my thumb. The scratch barely broke the skin. Later, my thumb hurt. Because of this, I concluded I had rabies.

Now, I knew I didn't have rabies. I'm not completely divorced from reality. But at the same time, I was absolutely sure I had rabies. I had never been more certain of anything in my entire life. I was sitting with Meg, calmly watching TV, and in the back of my head making end-of-life plans and deciding whether my family would have time to fly out to say goodbye to me. The division in my mind scared me. That I could know something was true (obviously I didn't have rabies) and yet at the same time believe with utter conviction that its opposite was true (I'm about to die I'm about to die I'm about to die), was terrifying. I truly felt, for the first time, like I no longer had control over my mind. I've had issues with severe anxiety for years, but this was the first time I felt something like what a cruel outsider might call "crazy."

"You're sure I don't have rabies?" I asked Meg.

"I am one hundred percent sure," she said. And I had to let her certainty stand in for mine, because I had no capability of creating certainty within myself.

"I need help," I told Meg.

"Yes, you do," she said.

As it turns out, she did too.

The day of the van meltdown started like a lot of days on tour, only this one was easier because we woke up in our own bed at home in Los Angeles. Meg needed to pick up a large van at the Burbank airport car rental so she could shuttle the *Night Vale* tour group to their next destination. I drove her over in our little Los Angeles car that we had recently bought, and I dropped her off and went home to wait for her so we could have lunch together. A long time passed. Much longer than we had expected. Finally, she called me. She was sobbing so hard she could not form words. My immediate thought was that either she was profoundly injured or she had hit a person with the van and killed them. These were the two conclusions that most fit the facts I had. Finally, she pulled enough of herself together to explain that the car rental place insisted that she hadn't returned the last van the tour had rented (she had) and so therefore she was barred from renting any more cars. And they refused to help her clear the situation up. And some part of her, after six years of constant touring, after so long of being the one in charge of this chaotic machine zooming all over the country, that part of her just broke.

When I got back to Burbank, I found her sitting on the concrete floor of the parking structure, sobbing. "I can't do it," she kept saying. "I just can't do it." Of the two of us, she has always been the stronger one. It was devastating to see that exterior crack open, to see pure panic surge from within. We made our way back to the car rental desk, where the employees were sympathetic and not a little alarmed. It took another hour after I arrived, but they finally figured out that yes, she had in fact returned the last van. And they let her rent a new one.

Back at the house, the newly rented van in our driveway with Fancy Feast curled up napping underneath it, Meg and I talked. "I just can't do it anymore. I've hit my limit," she said.

"We need help," I said.

"Yes. We need help."

With these realizations about ourselves came the understanding that our lives were going to have to fundamentally change. We started to think about what life would look like after touring. It was hard to imagine. Our relationship for six years has been lived on the road, in hotel rooms and backstages, in restaurants where we searched desperately for a green vegetable on the menu, in vans where I put on a new podcast episode and let her know her exit was in five miles, in airplanes where she took the middle seat so I could take the window because I panic less when I can see the ground, in cities where we didn't speak the language, didn't know which way downtown was, didn't understand the coins that were given to us as change at the store. We had structured our life around this scattering. Neither of us knew what it would look like if we held still.

We discussed the possibility of selling our New York house and moving full-time to Los Angeles. If anything to do with television ever got through the labyrinth of meetings and executive notes, then I might have a day-to-day job there. Years ago, the success of *Night Vale* had thrown open a door, and we had stumbled through it into a new kind of life. Now we had a feeling of passing through another door, one that would once again fundamentally alter our lives, but this time it was us choosing to reach out and gently open that door, stepping through on our own terms.

Still, transformation is transformation, and no matter how much we try to make it gradual, change can often be experienced by the mind as violence.

At the heart of this sat the question of having kids. We had decided we wanted to have kids before we got married. But the age we set for ourselves to start trying arrived so much faster than we had thought it would. We were still in the whirlwind of touring the world, and the idea of having kids then seemed premature. So we put it off for another year, and then another year after that. Eventually it became apparent to us the obvious truth that, if we kept taking it year by year in this way, we were going to run out the clock on this possibility for our lives, and the decision would be made for us.

We set about deciding whether to have kids a second time. Not carelessly, as a yes thrown to the future for other versions of ourselves to catch, but as something we would have to live with right away. This made it much more difficult. We spent months vacillating, understanding the basic and horrifying truth of these two possible directions for our future: we would regret it either way. There would be times when, our freedom and our money and our privacy curtailed by children, we would regret having made the decision we made. That is, if not true for all parents, certainly something that would be true for us. But if we decided not to have kids, there would be times when the thought of the lives that might have been lived, of the connection and family that might have happened, would create its own kind of unbearable regret. There is no way out of this life without regret. Our sole choice is which kind of regret we want to be saddled with.

One concern of mine is that I don't like children. Not that I think they're inherently bad, but I don't find them particularly cute and I don't want other people's children near me. This might seem to be a pretty big problem, but the way I see it, they're not actually children for long. If the reason to have kids is that you love children, well, in the scope of your child's life, that phase will be a short fraction, and for the rest of it you will have a teenager and then an adult. I'm actually excited about a teenager and an adult. Once they have their own independent mind and I can talk with them, and argue with them, and share with them what I think is important, and learn from them what they think is important, that is the reward of it all. The coos of an infant don't stack up to that for me.

But my major concern was not about the potential child at all. It was about Meg and me. Every article about parenting had said that having kids changes you, and it changes your relationship, forever. And I love Meg's and my relationship. It's exactly where I want it to be. That is a delicate balance, one that if it were lost would be very sad for me. My worry about a child is that it would drive some distance or fracture between Meg and me that, while not ending our relationship, would never truly be repaired or bridged. That is a thought I can hardly stand. And it's what I wrestled with most during this time of decision.

Back and forth, we went. Back and forth.

Right as we were deciding about children, we made another decision. To write this book. It seemed like a fun project, one suited to our strengths. But the timing of it meant that we were looking through our history carefully right at the time when we were trying to decide about our future. I think most of us, when we think of our pasts, think in general terms, a big picture narrative leading to today. But taking it detail by detail, the story of these ten years is not the big picture of anything. It's a lot of little details, cascading into a life. Each day is as much a part of the story as any other.

I don't know what writing this book will do to our relationship. Seeing each other's essays after they were written, we squabble over differences in remembered detail. The order of events. The intention of the other person. It's a reminder that, as unified as we feel (and I notice how often I write "we" in these later chapters as interchangeable with "I"), we are in fact different people, and have experienced the last ten years in fundamentally different ways. A relationship does not erase disagreement. A relationship is a continual decision, each day, to keep going despite disagreement. A marriage is not one creature, but two, working in the best tandem they can manage.

What happens to us after the end of this book? Predictions of the future are never about the future, but an indirect portrait of the present. How could I, ten years ago, straight out of college, moving to a city I'd never visited, have predicted much of anything that happened next?

Maybe we have kids. Which means we tour less, and when one of us is on tour, there is even more a sense of a scattering, that we are stretched out with one part of ourselves at 30,000 feet or watching a cooking show in a Hampton Inn, and the other part of us is at home, with the family we love. I think I would be a good dad, maybe not out of a natural inclination toward child rearing, but by the same stubbornness that has aided me in my writing career. There would be work to do, and I would do it. I'm afraid of most other things, but I'm not afraid of hard work.

If we have kids, we might lose many of our non-kid-having friends. Not out of a conscious decision on anyone's part, but just that lives shift, and children aren't fun to be around if they aren't yours (and probably not even then, a good chunk of the time). I think through who might stick with us, and who might drift off. It feels like a goodbye before anything has happened, but even still I prepare myself for loss.

Or maybe we don't have kids. Maybe we can't, and we decide to give up somewhere in the arduous years of fertility treatments and adoption screenings. We stay as we are, except no one stays as they are. Our life continues to swerve in unpredictable ways. And we change, both of us individually, and the two of us as a couple, every single day, in ways so small and gradual that we don't notice them until we are looking at a photo of us from 2019 and thinking, *Who were these people? And what happened to them?*

After my father got his heart diagnosis, I remember sitting with him by his piano. "I always knew something like this would happen," he told me. "My life was so good. It was always so good. I knew eventually the other shoe would drop."

Now I know exactly what he meant. Because my life has been wonderful. In my early twenties, I met a woman who was the perfect match for me. We've had the easiest relationship it's possible to have, which is to say that it has never been completely easy, but it has never been a struggle. I lucked into the career I always wanted, and we got to live a life that went beyond my wildest dreams of what was possible for me. And now here I am, only thirty-three, with all of that behind me, and anywhere between sixty years and five minutes in front of me.

Yet I keep waiting for that other shoe. Because it *will* drop. Nothing is easy forever. All stories end, even the good ones. I only hope we get to keep telling this story for a little while longer.

We decided to have children.

As of this writing, neither of us has gotten it together to actually start seeing a therapist.

There is a picture of us walking on the High Line Park in New York in 2009. In the photo, we wrap our arms around each other, bundled in thick winter coats. Our faces aren't visible, but our heads lean toward each other, talking quietly with the urgent conspiracy of early love. Hanging over us is a billboard, advertising a whiskey or else a car or else perfume. The text on the billboard says: "All I need is all I've got." That slogan was true for us then, in the fervent grasping of our first months of love, when we didn't have much at all. I imagine it will be true for us in ten years, with a sprawl of life behind us, with more people in our family perhaps, but still building our world out of what is around us.

I imagine that, ten years from now, 2019 will feel like present tense. A decade passes so quickly.

Meg

Dear you who does not yet exist and may never exist,

Hi, it's me, your mother, writing to you from the past in the public forum of a published book about your parents' love story. That's a strange statement to make, but I am assuming, knowing your parentage, that you've experienced weirder.

"Men plan, God laughs" is a Yiddish proverb that haunts and delights me. I am not a man, I love to plan, and I don't believe in God. But I do believe in the humor of our universe. It's possible that this letter is all very funny now for reasons I do not yet know about and God is laughing his nonexistent divine ass off. It could be funny haha, or funny strange, or funny painful like the way you laugh about something sad and you're not sure why. The wires just got crossed. Comedy and tragedy are the closest of partners; they share the same toothbrush.

Let me start with some context about the world as we knew it in 2019. Our country was in the first (and hopefully only) presidential term of a fascist dictator. Our planet was rapidly deteriorating from the effects of unregulated climate change. People were dying and going bankrupt at the hands of our corrupt and broken healthcare system, and two thousand people have more money than the rest of the world combined. And yet your parents decided to bring you into this world. Maybe you hate us bitterly for making that choice; for that I am sorry but a world like the one I am describing survives on hope and you, my child, are that hope—hope that you will help make the world a better place. We wagered that you would be one of the good ones to take up your spade and do the work of making this world a more just place.

That's a lot of pressure, I know, but wait, there's more. You, if you exist, were very closely planned, debated, and painstakingly decided upon. I hope you find comfort in this fact. We really thought about whether you would be a good addition to the world and our family, and while we are not sure at the time of this writing, we decided that you are worth the risk. So not only did we create you as a hope to help save our world, we were not even all the way sure it was a good idea. Take a deep breath. We love you.

Here is how we came to the agreement to have you. Your father and I always said we wanted kids, but when it came time to make it happen, we kept pushing the timeline back. In 2019 we stopped moving the goalpost. Earlier this year I woke up in the middle of the night with an understanding of a new truth: I no longer was questioning whether or not I would try to have kids. I was going to try. In the middle of the night, in a strange Los Angeles Airbnb, was the moment I began firmly standing on this side of trying for children. The switch had flipped. I can't explain why other than that I was too frustrated with not knowing. I love plans. I need a plan always. I needed to make plans for you.

Before you start thanking me for making this huge choice for you, know that my reasoning was entirely selfish. I only get one human experience and humanity has the wild experience of parenthood on offer. I want to know this part of humanity. I want to know the pain of childbirth, the worry of being a mother, and the responsibility of adding another soul to this world. I wanted to know what my DNA looks like when whipped together with your very handsome father's.

It's strange that this selfish decision ultimately leads to a great deal of selflessness. I am aware of what is to come. I will have to give you all of me in order for you to survive, but I didn't bring you into this world for you. I did it for me. It had to start with me doing this for myself because I am the only thing I can ever have complete faith in. You probably know this about me by now, but I like to be in charge. I like to be the one who makes the plans and takes responsibility for their successes and their failures. I like to be the one holding (or dropping) the ball.

Which is not to say I have no faith in your father. I have a great deal of faith in him and in our relationship. I think he will be a good father. Although, I do worry he will leave you on the roof of the car or come back from picking you up at preschool with the wrong child. I decided not to worry too much about those things because I know he will be really good at the parenting stuff where it counts. He's also more stubborn than a child could ever be, so I know he will be able to handle whatever unreasonable tantrums you throw at him. I would not add another person to this world with him if I didn't believe completely that he would help teach you to make the world a better place. He is a better person than me, and hopefully you are a better person than us both.

After finding my own clarity, I began the process of convincing your father that it was time to start planning for you. I told him that I felt in 2020 we should start to get serious about having you. The conversation we started having was the same circular one we have had many times over about kids. Yes, we do want kids, but do we reeeeallly want kids? Maybe we could just move to Hawaii and get a bunch of dogs and that would be enough? The world is too scary and deteriorating a place to bring another life into, is it amoral to repro-duce in *these times*? We don't really like kids. Would we like you? Our lives are full of adventure and travel that can only be afforded to us if there's nothing at home holding us back. Would our careers stall? Then after all those questions, I told him the answer: we were no longer going to be having that conversation. We need to forget about the Hawaiian dogs. There is no longer a *will-we/won't-we* conversation. The new conversation is *we will*, and now it's time to have new conversations. We started having conversations about home births, raising you Jewish, sending you to public school, whether we would yell at you a lot, whether you would celebrate Christmas, and who would take care of you if we weren't around. He was onboard—reluctant and terrified, but onboard.

Your father and I had our conversations about planning for you, and soon it became time to invite others in on our plan. This summer we started the slow and uncomfortable process of coming out to all of our childless friends, telling them that we wanted to have kids. We have been in this very cool club with them for years—the adults-with-no-kids club, who travel and stay out late and get invited out for drinks. We are unenthusiastic about handing in our membership.

In July after spending a ridiculously fun weekend on the Jersey shore complete with swimming in the ocean, lots of drinks, mini golf, and a rock concert with our dear friend Kate, I blurted out to her, "We are going to try to have a baby next year and you have to still be friends with us." She took it better than expected but did not succumb to my peer pressure of "You should have one too. So we don't have to do this alone." We have traveled all over the world with Kate, swam in fancy pools in Nice, truffle hunted in Tuscany, and held koalas in Brisbane. We joked that in 2050 we will take a vacation to the moon. What does it mean to add a child or children to that? Will you be pissed when we don't take you to the moon with us because we want to go with your fun Aunt Kate?

I don't want you to feel like we gave up our wild and wonderful life just for you. Maybe you will come to the moon with us and your Aunt Kate won't mind. I'm being honest with you, I haven't met you yet, but know that I'm completely comfortable taking the bet that you will be worth it. Also, while our lives have been great, there's a lot I am ready to give up. If I never have to try to park a 23 ft. long tour van in a busy downtown city right when a major sporting event lets out and I have to pee ever again, then you will have been worth it.

In winter of this year we started renting a small house in Los Angeles to get through the cold New York winter. I fell in love with LA after many, many attempts. It was finally right for me. I ate my words about that city and gave it a chance, and it's the most at home I've ever felt. I wonder if we end up raising you in LA or New York or both or maybe somewhere completely different. I go back and forth on this. A childhood in LA would give you access to so much. LA is an abundantly diverse place with so much culture and opportunity, but it's fast-paced and I worry it would put pressure on you to grow up fast—to grow up seeking fame over happiness. The Hudson River Valley is not a diverse place to grow up, but the air will be cleaner, the pace will be slower, and I have a better chance of protecting you from the ugliness of big-city life.

One of the reasons we moved to LA was so we could be closer to our friends, and we have so many friends here. We don't have that in New York; our life is isolated up there and quiet. It serves as a balance from our hectic lives on tour where we interact with thousands of people. When we stop touring, will that balance be wrecked? Will we feel alone? Will our little family be enough? Again, more pressure to add to you and fodder for your therapist(s).

I really hope that you get to know my parents. One of the reasons I struggled with where to raise you is because I want you to be close to them. I love my parents very much. Hopefully, you know them, and you love them too. They are the reason you exist for so many reasons. Number one being basic biology; their DNA is scrambled into yours forever with all the good and bad that comes with that. I hope you have their intelligence, their reasoning skills, their compassion and thoughtfulness. I hope that the boiled-over anger stops with me. I hope that disordered eating stops with me. I hope that if you are a girl you do still get that one random chin hair though—it connects you back to all the tweezers-wielding women who came before.

I got my annual physical and then a follow-up with a cardiologist because I want to make sure my body is in good shape before you live in it. I can't stand having company when the house is a mess, the same goes for this. After lots of tests the cardiologist said I was probably fine and to come see him again in five years, and I will. Maybe you'll be with me. If for some reason I'm not around anymore when you read this, there's probably a lot I'd like you to know about life. I'm not going to list all of that here. I trust that your father can tell you, or your new stepmom can. I assume your father was instantly remarried to a Jewish woman with large breasts within weeks of my departure. I'm sure she's great. You can always ask all your grandparents or aunts for advice or help. I know they will give you whatever you need; they always did for me. I'll see to it that you always have a pair of your own cowboy boots. I'm planning to be around, but I know, after years of planning for everything, that plans are just best guesses and you will guess wrong sometimes.

Your dad and I listened to a podcast episode, because of course we did, about the questions you should ask before having children. The questions were big picture and small picture. We spelled out our priorities and how we wanted to raise you. We agreed that our relationship was the most precious thing we have in life and we were going to protect that in every choice we made in parenting. This may seem unfair to you, but your father loved me first and really put the work in.

I'm a great deal of work at the time of writing this letter. I had a tremendously bad day at work a few weeks ago, and your father had to come and get me. He came and picked me up from the concrete floor of the Burbank airport parking garage where I was having a mental breakdown. At this point I have been on tour for almost six years and been in charge of those tours for five. Touring, just like life, is filled with moments where things go wrong and problems need to be solved. I am very good at that problem solving. On this day I wasn't. The snowball rolling down the hill caught up to me, and I lost myself in it. My brain scrambled stresses about missing shipments of merchandise, overfilled guest lists, insurance bills, piles of emails, and shouting jokes into big rooms full of people. It felt like they all hit me at once. I started crying and couldn't stop in the Budget Rental Car office, because there was a problem with a rental van I couldn't figure out how to solve. Your dad came and got me. Fixed the problem and took me home. After four hours I stopped crying, drove to the theater, and did a show. The next morning, I got up and drove to the next tour stop because the show must go on. Now I am certain that I can't go on with the show much longer. I am ready for new work. I am ready for you to join our family, and not just so I have an excuse to not live in vans and hotels anymore. But because I only get one life and I want to spend it with you and your father, and not alone on the floor of the Burbank airport parking garage.

There is so much unknown in our lives right now as we prepare to turn another page. I don't know if I can get pregnant. I don't know that I can survive childbirth. I don't know what you will be like. I don't know what type of mother I will be. I don't know what my career will be like. I don't know what type of world I will be bringing you into. A scary place, likely. For someone who thrives on planning, this is an uneasy position to be in. I am sustaining myself on the resoluteness of my choice to have you, on committing to a big plan, the biggest one of my life.

I wanted to conclude this book with a letter to you, so that you would know exactly what our lives were like before you came along and just how much career glory, great vacationing, and leisure time we sacrificed to give you your chance on this planet. Not really, but please remember that when we ask you to do chores that we could very well be in Hawaii with a team of beagles right now, and you could be a non-thing. I know that this letter puts a lot of pressure on you, and it should. Hopefully, you are like your parents and you thrive under pressure. Hopefully, unlike your parents, you know when to say when and won't let that pressure hurt you.

You, if you exist, now know your parents' love story, or at least the first part of it. You know that they grew up together and built a life together as equal partners. Maybe we will write another book in ten years about all the changes and stories we have gone through. Maybe we won't. But I do know how much I love my husband—your father, my best friend, my partner—and how building the movable home of our love has been the best way to spend the past decade.

Love always,
Your mother

P.S. I'm hoping you were born on Halloween. Either way, your father and I still plan on raising you goth.

Acknowledgments

THANK YOU TO OUR parents Jack and Lydia Bashwiner and Ron and Kathy Fink, to our sisters Anna Pow and Kate Zambarano, and to our "like a sisters" Allison Bane, Erika Kiel, and Kat Gibbons. Thank you to Jessica Cerovich, who was Joseph's first friend in New York and asked if she could be in this book. Yes you can, Jessica.

To our *Night Vale* crew, Jeffrey Cranor, Cecil Baldwin, Jon Bernstein, Symphony Sanders, Hal Lublin, Andrew Morgan, Mara Wilson, Molly Quinn, Jasika Nicole, Nathalie Candel, Danny Schmidt, Carrie Elkin, Mary Epworth, Lauren O'Neill, Dessa, Aby Wolf, Mal Blum, Erin McKeown, Dane Terry, Jason Webley, Eliza Rickman, Emma Frankland, Ezra Reaves, Emily Pojman Mirsky, Sarah Conboy, Lucy Goldberg, and Joella Knap. There's no one with whom we'd rather browse the gas station beef jerky aisle.

To Dylan Marron for marrying us and sitting with us at City Hall as we waited to get our marriage license for three hours when all the computers broke.

Jill Beckman, Desiree Burch, Kevin R. Free, Katy May Hudson, Kate Jones, Jacquelyn Landgraf, Erica Livingston, Daniel Mirsky, Rob Neill, Lauren Parrish, Joey Rizzolo, Kyra Sims, Adam Smith, and all the New York Neo-Futurists past, present, and future.

Also and always: our grandparents, aunts, uncles, cousins, niece and nephews, Marcy Braidman, Aliee Chan, Gaby Dunn, Glen David Gold, Susan and Scott Kobler, Jen Leavitt, Lianne O'Shea, Robbie Rainin, Francine Schott, Jillian Sweeney, Sara Shay, Bettina Warshaw, the Largo, the Bell House, the Kraine Theater box office, Stillwater,

ACKNOWLEDGMENTS

Oblong Books, and that really good falafel place in Hudson, New York, that closed a few years back.

To Mary Gaule and the entire Harper Perennial team, who shepherded this book through a very difficult year in all our lives.

And of course to our agent, Jodi Reamer, thank you for being excellent at your job and excellent in all things, and thank you for buying us garlic cheesy bread.

About the Authors

MEG BASHWINER is a writer, performer, tour manager, podcaster, and producer. She is the emcee for the international touring live show of the *Welcome to Night Vale* podcast. She is an alumni member of the acclaimed New York theater company the New York Neo-Futurists. She lives in the Hudson River Valley and Los Angeles with her husband.

JOSEPH FINK created the *Welcome to Night Vale* and *Alice Isn't Dead* podcasts, and cowrote the *New York Times* bestselling novels *Welcome to Night Vale, It Devours!,* and *Alice Isn't Dead.* He lives in the Hudson Valley and Los Angeles with his wife.